FORSAKING
ALL
OTHERS

FORSAKING ALL OTHERS

A True Story of
Interracial Sex and Revenge
in the 1880s South

CHARLES F. ROBINSON

THE UNIVERSITY OF TENNESSEE PRESS / KNOXVILLE

Library of Congress Cataloging-in-Publication Data

Robinson, Charles F. (Charles Frank)
Forsaking all others: a true story of interracial sex and revenge in the
1880s South / Charles F. Robinson. — 1st ed.
p. cm.
Includes bibliographical references and index.
ISBN-13: 978-1-57233-724-4 (hardcover: alk. paper)
ISBN-10: 1-57233-724-9 (hardcover: alk. paper)
1. Bankston, Isaac, d. 1884.
2. Bradford, Missouri.
3. Men, White—Southern States—Biography.
4. African American women—Southern States—Biography.
5. Southern States—Race relations—History—19th century.
6. Bankston, Isaac—Trials, litigation, etc.
7. Miscegenation—Southern States—Case studies.
8. Passing (Identity)—Southern States—Case studies.
9. Desha County (Ark.)—Biography.
10. Memphis (Tenn.)—Biography.
I. Title.

F220.A1R63 2010
306.84'608996073076819—dc22
2010019339

CONTENTS

ACKNOWLEDGMENTS

The writing of any manuscript is always to some extent a community effort. This book is no exception. There were a number of individuals who greatly affected the final product. Beth Juhl and Andrea Cantrell, librarians at the University of Arkansas, were reliable sources for me in my attempts to locate literature related to the subject. Daniel J. Ross, the director of the University of Alabama Press, offered many suggestions for improving the work. Although that press decided against accepting the work, I really appreciate Daniel's careful assessment of the manuscript. I must also pay homage to the former chair of the Department of History at the University of Arkansas, Jeannie Whayne, who gave me the research funding to take on this project. And I would like to thank Gene Adair, copyeditor at the University of Tennessee Press, for doing a great job in making the manuscript much more readable.

In my personal life, Reynelda Augustine deserves much of the credit for encouraging me to persevere despite the many moments of frustration that were tied to trying to find a scholarly press to embrace this study. Of course, my parents, Charles and Mary Robinson, and siblings, Tammy and Eric Robinson, were constant sources of support as well. Furthermore, I give all praises to God and his son, Jesus Christ, who enable me to fulfill my aspirations.

This book is dedicated to my three wonderful children—my sons, Charles and Jalen, and Chloe Augustine Jefferson.

INTRODUCTION

On January 24, 1884, Frederick Douglass, the famed black statesman and former abolitionist, shook the pillars of convention by wedding his white secretary, Helen Pitts, in a private ceremony held at the home of a Washington, D.C., minister. When news of the nuptials became public, a storm of criticism poured down on the couple from blacks and whites alike. Because of his celebrity, most of this scorn was directed toward Douglass. African Americans described Douglass's actions as irrational, contemptuous of black women, and indicative of his desire to abandon the black community. Whites vilified Douglass's character, labeling him a "lecherous old African Solomon" and declaring his marriage "a deliberate challenge to the Caucasian race." Even Douglass's children from his longtime marriage to his first wife, Anna, who had died in 1882, joined the chorus of disapproval, expressing sentiments that they would retain even after their father's death in February 1895.[1]

Although society largely condemned Douglass and Pitts for formalizing their interracial relationship, the couple seemed to suffer little as a result. Married in the District of Columbia, an area free from the legal restrictions of anti-miscegenation laws, and insulated by Douglass's notoriety and wealth, Douglass and Pitts went on to live out the remainder of their time together, traveling to Europe, attending formal functions stateside, playing croquet on the lawn of their home, and even dining with an American president.[2] Compared to the experiences of many other interracial couples of their time, the ease with which Douglass and

Pitts handled the opposition to their union was atypical. More often than not, such couples had to battle not only hostile public opinion but also belligerent individuals and judicial systems determined to punish and separate them.

In an attempt to better illuminate the often desperate circumstances that characterized many interracial relationships in the South during the post-Reconstruction period, this book examines the lives of Missouri Bradford and Isaac Bankston, an Arkansas couple who maintained a relationship for several years and married approximately one month before Douglass and Pitts did. Missouri and Isaac's experiences reveal how interracial couples managed, often adroitly, to negotiate the many obstacles designed to discourage them from formalizing their unions. Their saga also demonstrates how, despite such couples' best efforts, the southern racial atmosphere, social norms, and legal system made it virtually impossible for them to sustain their intimacy once it became public knowledge.

I chose Missouri and Isaac's story principally because, like so many other interracial couples in the South, they were relatively obscure figures. The 1880 federal census reveals that the twenty-year-old Missouri was a mulatto housekeeper, living and working in the home of a wealthy white merchant.[3] The same census lists Isaac as a forty-seven-year-old white farmer and sheriff. In fact, it was only because Isaac had won an elective county office that local papers reported on this interracial couple in any substantive way.[4] That newspapers took an interest in the union of Missouri and Isaac proved critical in my efforts to flesh out their experiences and place them in historical context.

Yet, the evidence available for reconstructing this couple's story is admittedly limited. In writing this book, I was forced several times to make educated guesses about the motivations and actions of the central figures, relying on well-established scholarship that has traced how men and women in similar circumstances comported themselves. However, despite such limitations, I believe that there is still sufficient evidence to render an important and interesting historical sketch of these people's lives. Also, I feel that it is imperative for historians to move beyond the stories of the powerful and articulate and to venture deeper into the lives of those deemed insignificant and common. By telling Missouri and Isaac's story, I seek to enlarge the effort to make historical study more encompassing and meaningful.

The book is divided into six chapters. Chapter 1 traces the life of Isaac and the Bankston family from the 1830s through the Civil War period. Coming of age in the antebellum Mississippi Delta, Isaac was subject to a thoroughly traditional southern socialization, and his early years give no hint that he would one day find himself emotionally involved with a woman of color.

In chapter 2, I continue my exploration of Isaac's life, following his migration across the Mississippi River into Desha County, Arkansas. During Reconstruction, Isaac formed important economic and political alliances with black Republicans, culminating in a successful bid for county sheriff. In this chapter, I also introduce Missouri for the first time, depicting her formative years in Mississippi and mapping her journey across the river into Arkansas City, the seat of Desha County. In addition, I show how fate and socioeconomic factors brought Missouri and Isaac together.

Chapter 3 analyzes how and why Missouri and Isaac's relationship blossomed and evolved. I explain the reasons that influenced the couple to move their relationship from an informal to a formal one. This chapter also investigates antimiscegenation laws, demonstrating the ways in which southern states enforced them and how interracial couples circumvented them.

Chapter 4 follows Missouri and Isaac to their new home in Memphis, Tennessee. Because their relationship had become too conspicuous, the couple felt compelled to leave Arkansas City for an area they believed would allow them greater freedom to associate with each other. Missouri and Isaac were married while in Memphis, and this unleashed the fury of a southern society bent on severely punishing them for what was considered a great social indiscretion.

In chapter 5, I detail how the couple was formally charged for violating the Tennessee antimiscegenation law. Isaac was arrested, jailed, and placed on trial. During the proceedings, Isaac challenged his social racial construction. His actions during the trial saved him from a conviction but made him a virtual outcast from southern white society.

Chapter 6 scrutinizes the public shame that Isaac felt as a result of his trial and how it drove his determination to avenge his lost honor. He returned to Arkansas City to confront the individual whom he held most responsible for injuring his reputation. Resorting to violence, Isaac sought to attain a measure of social redemption.

Although Missouri and Isaac's story cannot represent the totality of the experiences of southern interracial unions, it does illustrate the profound complexity of human beings who attempted to manifest their individuality amid powerful social pressures driving them towards conformity. This couple's narrative reminds us that throughout American history, common people routinely summoned personal courage to realize their aspirations against formidable odds. In doing so, these everyday Americans exposed the flaws in the society of their own times. Their examples encourage us all to remain committed to fostering personal rights in the present.

MISSISSIPPI ON HIS MIND: ISAAC BANKSTON'S FORMATIVE YEARS

For most of the residents of Arkansas City, Arkansas, the morning of May 6, 1884, was like so many others. High humidity greeted the sunrise, signaling the steadily increasing temperatures of the season. A light breeze blew through the soft leaves of tall maples. The melodious morning songs of small birds mixed with the crows of roosters announcing daybreak. Even in the early hours, many townspeople were already on the move. Workers at Crawford and Bullock Grocers swept dirt from the wooden walkway into the dusty streets. On a soon-to-depart steamboat docked on the nearby Mississippi River, a loud bell excitedly rang while chanting roustabouts loaded the boat with flour, sugar, cotton, corn, and other supplies. It was the chorus of a new dawn in Arkansas City, but Isaac Bankston could hear none of it. His troubled mind was doubtless filled with reflections on his present predicament and the course his life had taken. The once proud and popular sheriff of Desha County, Isaac now sat alone in a jail cell that he had once overseen. Gone was the prestige of a job that had made him one of the big men in the county. Gone was his reputation for honesty, sobriety, and respectability. And gone was the freedom that had allowed him to have two families—

one legitimate, the other illegitimate; one white, the other black.[1]

Although Isaac Bankston was born in Chicot County, Arkansas, in 1833, his earliest memories were probably of life on the family farm in Bolivar County, Mississippi. Isaac's father, Ignatius, and his mother, Rosa, had moved him, along with a family of five others, into that area sometime in 1838.[2] The county had only recently been organized, and streams of families, mostly from other parts of the South, poured into it to take advantage of the rich alluvial soils. The Bankstons probably crossed the Mississippi River at Napoleon, Arkansas, arriving in the town of Prentiss before moving to county lands farther east. Once settled, the Bankstons, like their neighbors, labored to clear the land in preparation for growing the principal staple of the region: cotton.[3]

Surviving and prospering in the Mississippi Delta during antebellum times was no mean feat. The Bankstons encountered a demanding frontier. Seasonal rains often caused the Mississippi to overflow its banks, flooding lands that were already low and swampy in many places. The stifling heat and humidity contributed to the spread of cholera and dysentery, while mosquitoes left malaria and yellow fever in their wake. Some areas abounded with trees and thick brush that were extremely difficult to clear. The Delta even had its fair share of dangerous wild panthers and bears.[4]

Despite the perils, most white families moved to the Mississippi Delta because they saw promise in the land's fertility. Many settlers had left farms with depleted soils, and in their eyes the Delta's lands offered a chance to maintain or enhance their economic standing.[5] This, in all probability, was what motivated the Bankstons to migrate to Bolivar County. New political opportunities were likely another compelling factor.[6]

The Mississippi legislature had organized Bolivar County in 1836. Thus, when the Bankstons arrived two years later, the county government was still in a fledging state. This afforded Ignatious Bankston an opportunity to build a political career. Coming of age in the era of Jacksonian Democracy, common white men like Ignatius Bankston felt they had every right to a political voice. And just one year after Ignatius's relocation to Mississippi, Bolivar County residents elected him to the Third Board of Police, a five-man governing body that oversaw county business. In 1842 Ignatius ran successfully for county assessor—an office in which he never served because of his failure to make bond. (Municipalities and counties often required winning candidates to put money into the local coffers as insurance against corruption; if the candidate personally lacked the required sum, he could still secure backing from wealthy local citizens.) Despite the initial setback to his political ambitions, however, Bankston reemerged in local politics in 1854, when he won the position of county treasurer, a post he probably kept until the Civil War.[7]

The Bankstons also moved to Bolivar County because Lafayette Bankston, Ignatius's brother, had settled there in 1837. The brothers likely thought that they could help one another develop the land that each would eventually acquire. In 1850 the census reported that both Ignatius and Lafayette Bankston had purchased approximately 160 acres of land. By 1860 Ignatius's holdings, with a taxable value of $794, were a bit more lucrative than those of Lafayette, which were valued at $476.[8]

To cultivate their land, the Bankstons relied mostly on family labor. Ignatius's family owned no slaves in 1850 and only one in 1860.[9] Lafayette purchased his only slave around 1855.[10] Possibly, the Bankston family hired slave laborers to assist with some of the work, but like many of their Bolivar County neighbors, the Bankstons used children and extended family to do most of the labor on the farm.[11] The 1840 census revealed that only three people in Ignatius Bankston's household worked as agricultural laborers. However, by 1850 Ignatius's household consisted of twelve people: Ignatius; his wife, Rosa; Isaac; a daughter, Barthema; four other sons, John, William Lafayette, Thomas Jefferson, and James; and a woman named Mrs. Hildah Davis and her three children, Sarah, Thomas, and Elizabeth, who were likely tenants. Of the twelve household members, at least seven were old enough (the standard being ten years and above) to work in the fields. Lafayette Bankston lived on a nearby farm with his wife, Angeline, and their two-year-old child.[12]

In July 1850 Rosa Bankston died.[13] The cause of her death is unknown, but whatever it was, her passing no doubt placed a severe strain on the family because of the vital role she played. The wives of southern yeoman farmers like Ignatius Bankston worked both inside and outside of the house. Lacking the benefits of the slave labor enjoyed by the plantation mistress, nonelite women raised subsistence crops, cooked, cleaned, made homespun clothes, and were the principal caretakers of younger children. Nonelite women could also be found on occasion working beside their husbands in the fields. Rosa Bankston's death meant that some other woman in the household would have to assume her role.[14]

Although untimely death was a common occurrence on antebellum farms, the losses were no less traumatic for these families. Rosa had been married to Ignatius for over twenty years and was a mother to no fewer than eight children, one of whom had not survived early childhood. Isaac Bankston, the oldest living male child, would have been particularly pained by the loss of his mother. Rosa likely had assigned him some responsibility for the care of his younger siblings. As he aged, Isaac would have been the first of the children sent on errands by Rosa to neighboring farms. He would have been the first of the children assured a formal education. Although southern girls sometimes received the rudiments of education, antebellum southerners placed greater emphasis on educating boys because they believed that their sons would have the weightier obligation of providing for their families. Rosa would have also looked to Isaac to help in protecting the reputation of his sisters. Southern honor codes demanded that the males of the family defend the public reputations of female members. Under his mother's instruction, Isaac probably accompanied his sisters on outings away from the farm, and his presence would have been even more prominent when his sisters began courting suitors.[15]

Finding a permanent replacement for Rosa would not have been easy. The temporary role of family caretaker possibly fell to either Barthema Bankston or Hildah Davis. However, by 1860 both of them had left the Bankston household. In their stead, a new woman had emerged as the family matriarch. In August 1858 Isaac Bankston married Martha Elizabeth White, a seventeen-year-old white woman who had also migrated from Arkansas to Mississippi with her family.[16]

Isaac Bankston's decision to take a wife may have been tangentially tied to the loss of his mother. If Barthema Bankston and Hildah Davis left the Bankston household prior to Isaac's marriage to Martha, the Bankstons would have been left without a maternal caretaker. Of course, Ignatius could have remarried, but as a man in his fifties, he might have been reluctant to do so. None of the other Bankston men appear to have been old enough to take that step. Thus, at least part of Isaac's decision to marry in 1858 may have been linked to an attempt to restore relative normality to the Bankston household.

By 1860 the Bankston household had dwindled to six members, the youngest being fifteen-year-old Thomas Jefferson Bankston. This meant that each of the Bankston family members contributed labor to the farm. Yet, because the Bankstons had acquired more land, they also purchased a slave. The Bankstons left no family records with details about the identity of their slave. Nor did census takers provide substantial information about him. The 1860 slave schedules failed even to provide the names of slaves. All that is known of the Bankston slave is that he was a thirty-year-old male.[17]

Being the only slave of a white family meant that the Bankston slave's experiences differed in significant ways from those of slaves laboring on plantations or larger farms. He had no slave community living with him, and while it is possible that he had a wife and children on a nearby farm, he would have spent more time away from them than with them. The Bankston slave probably lived in the barn rather than in the traditional slave quarters. He probably knew each of the Bankstons and shared idle conversation with them. The Bankston slave worked alongside his masters without a regular overseer or slave driver, and because of this closeness, the Bankstons may have considered him to some extent part of the family.[18]

It is doubtful that the Bankstons had any moral qualms about owning a slave. Throughout their lives, they had always lived in areas heavily populated by slaves and had come to know slavery as a central part of southern culture. In fact, the Bankstons may even have wanted to own more slaves but simply could not afford them, since a prime male field hand could cost upwards of two thousand dollars. Although the Bankstons had not owned any slaves prior to the 1850s, the family would have been well aware of the southern social mores that governed the interactions between whites and blacks. The Bankstons would have expected their slave to address them with respect and to keep his eyes down while doing so. The family no doubt frowned at the idea of teaching their slave how to read and write. Furthermore, they would have expected him to defer to their judgment and opinions in almost every matter.[19]

The Bankstons would also have been aware of the political crisis of the 1850s. Mississippi, a Deep South state with a slave majority, had many so-called fire-eaters who longed to secede from the Union and establish a separate slaveholding confederacy. Every national episode involving the issues of slavery and states' rights—the California statehood crisis, the Kansas-Nebraska controversy, the *Dred Scott* decision—emboldened them and added fuel to the secessionist fires. Moderate leaders struggled to keep the state in the national fold. However, as the sectional crisis worsened, these moderates steadily lost their grip on Mississippi politics.[20]

In 1859 the state Democratic Party chose a slate of secessionist candidates, including John Jones Pettus—described as "a disunion man of the most unmitigated order"—for the office of governor. Throughout the decade, Pettus had opposed all compromises on sectional issues. One month before the election, a coalition representing the crumbling Whig and Know-Nothing parties announced its own candidates. Chief among them was the gubernatorial contender, Harvey W. Walter, a prominent lawyer who favored moderation in the sectional crisis. Although the wealthiest planters in the state traditionally favored the Whigs, by 1859 the vast majority of Mississippi voters were casting their lot with the Democrats. Pettus won by a landslide, securing 34,559 votes out of the 44,882 cast. Walter carried only three counties: Bolivar, Tishomingo, and Warren.[21]

Despite the success of the fire-eaters in the 1859 election, the Union cause was not completely lost in the state. There was still enough moderate sentiment in the legislature to make passing an ordinance of secession a very hard fight. Also, at the national level, some Mississippi leaders—including planter Jefferson Davis, a United States senator and future president of the Confederacy—supported compromise solutions to the sectional imbroglio. However, John Brown's raid against a U.S. arsenal in Harpers Ferry, Virginia, destroyed much of the already waning optimism of southern moderates. In October 1859 Brown, an ardent abolitionist, initiated the raid with the intent of seizing weapons and fomenting a massive slave insurrection. Although federal authorities quickly subdued Brown and his partisans, the episode sent the southern states into a sectional frenzy. One Mississippi newspaper, the *Aberdeen Sunny South,* accurately summarized the raid's significance by calling it "The Beginning of the End." Throughout the South, state legislatures began placing their militias on a war footing. Many southern moderates who had before been opposed to disunion now joined the secessionist camp out of fear that abolitionist groups were planning further insurrectionary ventures.[22]

Throughout the political crisis of the 1850s, the opinions of the Bankstons probably mirrored those of their neighbors, favoring moderation at the beginning of the decade and then hardening their stands as news and rumors of the growing northern threat reached them. One thing is certain: the Bankstons could not have escaped these issues. Events related to slavery and the sectional controversy would have been discussed in nearby towns such as Cleveland, Prentiss, and Greenville. Undoubtedly, the crisis became dinner and parlor-room conversation. The sectional controversy was everywhere, and the Bankstons had to have grappled with it.[23]

In 1860 anxiety about the future of the Union could only have increased in the Bankston household. As their candidate for president, the Republicans nominated Illinois attorney and onetime congressman Abraham Lincoln, who had gained national attention two years earlier in the highly publicized Lincoln-Douglas debates. Then a candidate for the U.S. Senate, Lincoln announced in those debates his opposition to the extension of slavery into the territories.

Many southerners interpreted Lincoln's position as an indirect threat to abolish slavery everywhere if he were elected to the nation's highest office.[24]

At the Democratic National Convention, party delegates could not unite on a candidate for the presidency. Northern Democrats generally threw their support to the influential senator from Illinois, Stephen Douglas. Southern Democrats rejected Douglas because of his equivocation on the slavery issue during his debates with Lincoln. In Freeport, Illinois, Douglas had suggested that territories could circumvent the Dred Scot decision by simply refusing to pass laws that offered protection to the institution: he knew that many northern voters opposed that part of the high court's ruling that strengthened slaveholders' rights in the territories. Instead of supporting Douglas, southern leaders bolted the party and chose John C. Breckenridge, the states' rights governor from Kentucky, as their presidential candidate. They also threatened to secede if Lincoln won the election.[25]

Lincoln, who had promised not to interfere with the institution of slavery in the South, won the election despite losing every southern state. The election results set off a rapid movement towards secession in Mississippi. Governor Pettus summoned the legislature to meet in special session to discuss the issue and subsequently requested a conference with the state's congressional delegation. With power in the legislature firmly in secessionist hands, a resolution declaring secession the only proper recourse under the existing circumstances was adopted. The legislature also called an election for December 20, 1860, to choose delegates to a state convention that would make the final decision on whether or not Mississippi would withdraw from the Union. When the convention convened on January 7, 1861, it had a secessionist majority. After spiritless debate, the secession ordinance passed. Following the lead of South Carolina, Mississippi declared itself an independent entity.[26]

Within weeks of the secession ordinance's passage, white citizens of Mississippi geared up for war. No fewer than eighty volunteer companies began organizing in the state. Governor Pettus also authorized the seizure of federal property—specifically, Fort Hill, which lay north of Vicksburg, and the naval works at Ship Island.[27] Similar activities were underway in the six other Deep South states that voted for secession. By the end of February, these states had formed a new government, the Confederate States of America, to represent the political interests of the South.

Despite all the preparation for war, as March approached neither North nor South had actually taken up arms against the other, and neither appeared in a hurry to do so. Furthermore, eight slave states had not seceded. President Lincoln hoped to hold these states in the Union, thus significantly reducing the power of the seceding states. However, events at Fort Sumter changed everything. During the early hours of April 12, 1861, Confederate batteries under General P. G. T. Beauregard began a forty-hour bombardment of the recalcitrant U.S. fort in Charleston Harbor. After Fort Sumter's surrender, President Lincoln called for seventy-five thousand volunteers to suppress "combinations too powerful to be suppressed by the ordinary course of judicial proceedings." Lincoln's action precipitated the withdrawal of four other slave states: Virginia, North Carolina, Arkansas, and Tennessee. The Confederacy was now complete, and the war had finally begun.[28]

The lull in the secession movement had placed considerable strain on the state of Mississippi. Because the spirit for war had been so strong immediately following the state's withdrawal from the Union, the Mississippi Military Board received more volunteers than the state could accommodate. The surrender of Fort Sumter served only to increase the furor. Governor Pettus, in an attempt to deal with this problem, sent companies of men to Pensacola, Florida, to assist in the capture of Fort Pickens. He also convinced the Military Board to stop accepting volunteers.[29]

The moratorium on enlistment went into effect on May 14, 1862. Lacking enough guns and other essentials to supply the already existing companies, Governor Pettus and the Military Board assumed that their decision would be well received statewide. They were wrong. Throughout the state people complained bitterly about the restrictive policy, and the Military Board rescinded the ban just one month after implementing it. By the end of July, the numbers of companies on state muster rolls increased to a new high of 125.[30]

In step with other Mississippi residents, William Lafayette Bankston volunteered his service to his state and the Confederacy in July 1861. He enlisted in Miles McGehee Rifles, a company raised in Bolivar County. By August this outfit was part of the Mississippi 20th Infantry Regiment.[31] That same month the regiment was sent to Virginia, where it earned the distinction of being the first

Mississippi unit to serve under the command of Robert E. Lee, the commander of the Army of Northern Virginia. The 20th Mississippi participated in battles mostly in western Virginia. Fighting in mountains throughout that campaign, the men in William's regiment were exposed to inclement weather and lacked adequate shelter and food.[32]

In December 1861 the Confederate War Department ordered the 20th Mississippi to Kentucky to reinforce General Albert Sidney Johnston. At Fort Donelson, the regiment distinguished itself, battling desperately to resist the Union forces' attempt to capture the fort. Yet, despite the efforts of the 20th Mississippi and other Confederate regiments, Fort Donelson fell to the Union troops on February 16, 1862. On that same day, William became one of the more than ten thousand soldiers captured and sent to federal prison camps.[33]

William was imprisoned at Camp Douglas, a sixty-acre compound located on the south side of Chicago. As one of the first Confederate soldiers to arrive at the prison, William probably found his accommodations adequate. One Confederate captive, Thomas A. Head of Tennessee's 16th Volunteer Regiment, reported that when the camp first opened, "the prisoners had kitchens supplied with stoves and cooking utensils and were supplied more provisions than they were able to consume." However, as a result of Union victories throughout the spring and summer of 1862, the prison population at the camp rose to nearly nine thousand. Conditions deteriorated rapidly. Lacking a proper sewer system, Camp Douglas was enveloped by a foul and suffocating stench and plagued with polluted drinking water. Inmates also suffered from cramped quarters and insect infestation. Such circumstances led to the spread of disease and an ever-increasing death rate.[34]

On March 9, 1862, within a month of William's capture, Ignatius joined Mayson's Dragoons. Isaac also enlisted in the Confederate army, joining the Washington Calvary. Both of these companies eventually became part of the 28th Mississippi Calvary.[35]

Generally, the experiences of the Bankstons as Civil War soldiers were not unlike those of other participants. As members of their respective regiments, the Bankstons came to know the harshness, misery, and drudgery of war. They encountered long hard marches through low marshy areas and up high hard terrain. They experienced days of hunger and endured nights of cold. They became all too familiar with the distinctive sound of minié balls whistling through the air and the cries of dying soldiers whose bodies had been torn by shrapnel.[36]

Also, the Bankstons confronted the fear of death and the agony associated with the loss of a loved one. Less than a year after volunteering for service, Ignatius Bankston died. Although no record indicates the reason for his passing or its exact date, evidence suggests that he died between October and November 1862 and that the cause may have been related to his advanced age. Ignatius had enlisted at the age of sixty. Considering that most Civil War soldiers were between eighteen and thirty years old, one can only imagine the difficulty of Ignatius's struggles to keep pace with the other men in his unit.[37]

Isaac would have been the first to learn of his father's death because of their service in the same regiment.

He received a brief furlough to handle Ignatius's affairs. William, having been released from Camp Douglas as part of a prisoner exchange, received news of Ignatius's demise while serving with his unit in Tennessee. Shortly thereafter, William accepted a reassignment to Company D in the 28th Mississippi Calvary. He wanted to serve nearer to his older brother.[38]

Unfortunately for William, he would not get the chance to endure the rest of the war with Isaac. Isaac's active duty with the 28th Mississippi came to a rather abrupt end in December 1863. His last company muster roll indicates that Isaac was ordered to Washington County, Mississippi, to a "mounted detached service."[39]

As it did for most southerners, the Civil War and southern defeat significantly changed the lives of the Bankstons. The conflict not only forced them apart for years, but it also permanently altered their family structure by taking the life of its patriarch. Although the strain of the war surely marked the faces of the family combatants upon their return from the service, those left behind had doubtless suffered as well.[40] Like so many other southern families, the Bankstons struggled to find food and other essentials.

The war brought tremendous economic challenges to the family. Slavery's collapse meant not only that the Bankstons had lost an asset worth thousands of dollars but also that the family would have to find ways to replace that labor. Furthermore, because Union soldiers had destroyed the levee that offered protection to Bolivar County lands from the Mississippi River's overflow, flooding had rendered much of the area useless by the conclusion of the war in April 1865.[41] Although this was prime planting season, the Bankstons would have to wait for the waters to recede before they could attempt to work the land.

At this important juncture in their family's journey, Isaac and Martha decided to set out on their own. In September 1865 the couple sold land inherited from Lafayette Bankston's estate and moved to Desha County, Arkansas. There Isaac and Martha would establish a new Bankston household and attempt to restart their lives.[42]

* * *

The story of the Bankston family from the antebellum years through the Civil War suggests that of a typical southern white yeoman family. The Bankstons had forged an existence on a difficult frontier, relied primarily on family labor, and saw their family grow both in number and in the value of its assets. The Bankstons appear to have named several of their children after prominent southern political leaders. James P. Bankston was probably named for James K. Polk, president of the United States during the year of James's birth in 1848. John C. Bankston's name likely came from that of John C. Calhoun, a prominent senator from South Carolina, and Thomas Jefferson Bankston clearly received the name of the third American president. Like so many other white southern families, the Bankstons endorsed slavery, the etiquette of race relations, and the states' rights position during the sectional crisis. When civil war came, the Bankstons fought, suffered, and died for Mississippi and the Confederacy.

Nothing in Isaac's known family history indicates that he would one day become involved in a tragic story of intimacy with a woman of color. However, the absence of any perceivable indicators of Isaac's eventual relationship with Missouri Bradford is nevertheless revealing. Isaac's very "commonness" suggests that for white southern men of the time interracial sex was not an aberration but a regular occurrence. They did not require special circumstances or have to posess unique characteristics to enter into affairs with women of color. Episodes of interracial sex with black women did not make these men any less traditional, nor did they put them out of step with the mores of their time. To the contrary, such liaisons placed white southern men squarely in pace with their era. It would be Isaac's decision to marry his black paramour that makes his story unique and worthy of a fuller investigation.

THE CONFLUENCE
ACROSS THE RIVER

Isaac and Martha arrived in an Arkansas that was in transition. Like blacks and whites throughout the South after the war, Arkansans sought to reclaim their lives and communities. They rebuilt cities and towns, repaired farms, and reestablished county and state governments. Southern Unionists in Arkansas had taken political charge of the state as early as January 1864. Empowered by federal military control of Little Rock, the state capital, and by President Lincoln's Reconstruction plan, Unionists drafted and approved a new constitution, elected legislators, and selected a new governor, Isaac Murphy of Madison County. The new state officials fell in line with Lincoln's requirement that slavery be abolished but went further by repudiating Confederate debt and denying the right of secession. Once in power, the new legislature passed a loyalty provision that denied voting rights to anyone who had aided the Confederacy since April 18, 1864, the date of the new governor's inauguration.[1]

With the end of the war in 1865, former Confederates in Arkansas began agitating for voting rights. Their demands for suffrage were assisted by two occurrences, one at the national level, the other at the state level. Nationally, Andrew Johnson's becoming president after Lincoln's assassination meant that southern whites had an ally in the White House. Johnson, a southerner, initiated a Reconstruction plan that returned political rights to most former Confederates who petitioned for them. Within Arkansas, conservative Democrats successfully challenged the state's loyalty oath provision through the courts. In *Rison et al v. Farr* (1865), the Arkansas Supreme Court ruled that the state constitution gave no power to the legislature to restrict the voting rights of adult white males.[2]

The political enfranchisement of former Confederates ensured their return to power in Arkansas politics. In August 1866 conservative Democrats took control of both houses of the state legislature. None of the Unionists standing for reelection were successful in their bids for office. Conservatives also seized power in most of the other states that had seceded from the Union. By the start of 1867, it appeared that former Confederates throughout the South had regained with the ballot box what they had lost on the battlefield.[3]

The reemergence of the former masters to positions of political power did not bode well for the civil rights of former slaves. In Arkansas conservatives enacted legislation that relegated blacks to inferior status. Arkansas legislators denied blacks voting rights and forbade them from serving on juries or in the state militia. In addition, the state outlawed intermarriage and authorized a segregated public school system.[4]

By January 1867 conservative Democrats seemed to have a firm grasp on state power. Nationally, however, events

were already in play that would severely weaken their hold. In the fall 1866 congressional elections, northern voters, wary of developments in the South, gave Republicans heavy majorities in both houses. Beginning in March 1867, Republicans passed new Reconstruction legislation over the vetoes of Andrew Johnson—acts that voided the existing state governments in all of the former Confederate states except Tennessee. The provisions then placed the ten remaining southern states in five military districts, putting military governors in charge of keeping the peace and registering adult males who were eligible to vote. Excluded from voting were those who had ever sworn allegiance to the U.S. government and then betrayed that oath by actively supporting the Confederacy. Once a state had constructed a new constitution and chosen new leaders, that state would then gain official readmission upon its ratification of the Fourteenth Amendment, a measure designed to both empower blacks and punish former Confederates.[5]

Radical Reconstruction, as the collection of new measures came to be known, ushered in an era of significant political and social change in the South. The Republican Party, nonexistent in the region before the war, now stood as a viable party. African Americans, enslaved and disenfranchised in antebellum times, became the primary constituents of southern Republicans. With their newfound political clout, white and black southern Republicans muscled through legislative provisions that expanded opportunities for African Americans and weakened the legal foundations for prewar notions of white supremacy.[6]

In Arkansas the racial leveling produced by Radical Reconstruction manifested itself in many ways. African

Americans served as delegates to the constitutional conventions of 1868 and 1874 and maintained a presence in every General Assembly until 1894. Also, the state implemented two civil rights laws. The 1868 statute forbade discrimination against blacks using public accommodations or public conveyances, while the 1873 provision echoed this same theme, utilizing stronger language.[7] In addition, the General Assembly passed a public school act that required black inclusion, and state authorities omitted anti-miscegenation laws from the revised civil codes in 1874.[8]

Isaac and Martha Bankston were likely aware of the political and social developments in the state. Throughout the Radical Reconstruction period, the Bankstons lived near Knowlton's Landing, a small town in the northwestern section of Desha County. Located in the Arkansas Delta, the county had a black majority. This meant that the Bankstons, like their white neighbors, would have witnessed blacks going to the polls for the first time. Also, the Bankstons were probably aware of the exploits of the state's prominent black politicians, such as William H. Grey and James T. White of neighboring Philips County and James W. Mason of nearby Chicot County. Within Desha County, the Bankstons certainly knew of black officeholders like James Baldwin, a twenty-eight-year-old farmer who served as justice of the peace in 1872.[9]

Although it is impossible to know how Isaac and Martha initially reacted to the enfranchisement of blacks, one can surmise that they were probably surprised and somewhat disturbed by it. The Bankstons had come of age during the antebellum era, when the vast majority of African Americans were slaves. Even any free blacks the

Bankstons might have known or heard of would have been largely marginalized by whites. Furthermore, the Bankstons had possessed at least one slave of their own. To see black people empowered during Reconstruction must have been shocking at first for the couple and required emotional adjustments.

However, in a relatively short time, Isaac had assimilated to the new political environment. By 1876 he had joined the Republican Party.[10] The evidence of Isaac's associations from 1865 to 1876 gives little indication of why he aligned with the Republicans. He may have been a Whig prior to the Civil War and blamed the Democrats for taking the South out of the Union, bringing the suffering of war to both the region and his family. Perhaps Isaac recognized the potential for Republican politicians in the county and thought that his interests would be better served by joining that party. Or, Isaac may have thought that he could work with other white southerners who had become Republicans and help them in refashioning the party's political agenda along the lines of traditional southern values.[11]

Isaac's decision to join the Republicans in 1876 is especially significant when examined in the light of statewide politics. By that time in Arkansas, Republicans had lost control of both the governor's office and the General Assembly. In 1874 Democrats had convened a constitutional convention and constructed a new state constitution. With Democrats in control of the state government, their influence was felt at the county level. In Desha and other Delta counties, fusion politics became the norm—arrangements whereby county Democrats and Republicans agreed to share power. The division of county authority also broke down along racial lines. Some of the Republicans elected to office were African Americans.[12]

From 1874 to 1890, southern Republicans accepted fusion politics in areas like the Arkansas Delta because they recognized the fragility of their political conditions. In Arkansas not only had conservative Democrats regained control of state politics but by 1874, on the national level, northern public support for Reconstruction was waning. It came as little surprise that after the disputed presidential election of 1876, Congress agreed to end Reconstruction with the Compromise of 1877. Now that federal troops were removed from the South, black Republican leaders realized that they would have to forge workable political relationships with white conservatives in order to stave off wanton violence. For their part, conservatives embraced fusion because of the overwhelming majorities that blacks held in Delta counties. Furthermore, Democrats were reluctant about moving too quickly to disenfranchise African Americans out of fear of rekindling federal involvement in southern affairs.[13]

In 1876 Isaac Bankston ran successfully for county sheriff. In that year, the Desha County Republicans were split into two factions, one led by Andy Robinson, a black farmer, and the other by J. Pennoyer Jones, a prominent black lawyer and businessmen. The Robinson group consisted of only black men, while the Jones list comprised white and black candidates. Isaac was part of the Jones clique.[14] The election results clearly reflected fusion politics. James P. Clayton, a local white Democrat and former member of the General Assembly, won the office of county judge. Meanwhile, at least two Republicans in addition to Isaac secured offices: Jones won the county clerk's race, and

George Wilson, a twenty-eight-year-old black grocer, was elected assessor.[15]

In April 1877, shortly after his election as sheriff, Isaac purchased 160 acres of farmland in Desha County. The land was originally part of 320 acres that Jones owned near Walnut Lake in the Jefferson Township, and Isaac bought it from him for $250.[16] This property transaction was significant for Isaac. Not only did the land give him a strong foundation from which to build his personal wealth, but it also further cemented his allegiance to Jones and the Republican Party. Moreover, these political and business dealings are evidence that Isaac's racial thinking had likely undergone modification. To Isaac, African Americans could be partners both politically and economically. It would not be long before Isaac would view at least one black woman as a partner of a different sort.

Isaac Bankston had many duties as county sheriff. He arrested people accused of crimes, summoned witnesses to trials and grand jury proceedings, and executed orders involving property disputes. He was also responsible for collecting county taxes. These varied jobs placed Isaac squarely in the public eye and gave him opportunities to build relationships with prominent men of both parties in the county. For example, he would have known Henry Thane, a successful businessman and a chairman of the Republican County Central of Desha County, who also served as a postmaster under Presidents Rutherford B. Hayes and Chester A. Arthur. In 1882 Thane won a seat in the state senate, and from 1886 to 1890 he served as the county clerk for Desha. Isaac's position placed him in direct contact with white Democrats such as B. F. Merrit and Benjamin McGehee. Merrit, elected county judge in 1882, was a wealthy real estate holder, planter, and lawyer, who also served as a notary. McGehee, a farmer and surveyor, won the post of county surveyor in 1882. Two years earlier, in August 1880, McGehee had secured a property judgment for which Isaac oversaw the implementation of the court ruling.[17]

Isaac's notoriety and popularity grew among Desha County residents during his tenure as county sheriff. Among his various duties, his office required him to assist county residents in times of need. Such was the case during the flood of 1882. In February and March of that year, heavy rains left much of the county under high water that destroyed crops, drowned livestock, forced countless people from their homes, and led to widespread starvation and death. Giant gnats that came in the wake of the storm added to the misery. So severe was the disaster that government assistance was required in the form of bread and meat. As sheriff, Isaac played a role in distributing this relief throughout the county.[18]

To his Desha County constituents and neighbors, Isaac was a rising star and model citizen who led an apparently idyllic life. By 1880 Isaac and Martha had two children: seven-year-old Isaac Jr. and six-year old Laura. The family built a home on their land and ran a profitable farming enterprise, which included seventy acres of improved land, two horses, four mules, fifteen cows, seven calves, and thirty pigs. The family grew mostly corn but also raised crops of cotton and potatoes. In addition, the Bankstons had four boarders, all black, who worked as laborers.[19]

Isaac Bankston was so popular and politically well connected that he won an unprecedented five consecutive terms as county sheriff. Isaac's considerable support was evidenced in a December 1882 article in the *Arkansas City Journal*. The newspaper reported that Isaac had filed a $38,000 bond in order to continue in his position as sheriff, although the law required much less; the amount was underwritten by "some of the best men of the county." Also, Isaac's name appeared among a list of important signatures on a letter to the General Assembly requesting county control of swamp and overflow lands so that a levee could be constructed.[20] Yet, Isaac's public image masked a private reality that would eventually lead to his downfall. What the public did not know was that at the zenith of Isaac Bankston's success, he had entered into a relationship with Missouri Bradford, a black woman who did not fit into his public white world.

* * *

Historical records scarcely mention Missouri Bradford. What little is known of her comes largely from the 1880 census and a series of articles published by the *Arkansas Gazette* about her relationship with Isaac Bankston. However, by taking the limited documentation of her life and combining it with what is known about the general conditions of black women in similar circumstances, one can construct a likely composite of who Missouri was and how she felt about her dealings with Isaac.

The census described Missouri as a mulatto.[21] Because her birth occurred at the onset of the Civil War, there is no way to know for certain when her family and she obtained freedom. Federal troops came to western Mississippi as early as the fall of 1862 and were a significant presence by 1863. Missouri's family may have been among the thousands who rushed to Union lines in search of freedom. Or, they may have remained slaves over the course of the war.[22]

Life after emancipation for Missouri and her family could not have been easy. Being thrust into a market economy with no capital or education meant that Missouri's family had only their bodies to trade. Like many other former slaves, Missouri's parents probably aspired to own land and believed that the federal government would provide them with titles to some acreage. However, the hope for land ownership would go unrealized for most freedmen. Moreover, the conservative Mississippi legislature further limited the economic choices of former slaves by passing laws that would ensure their status as laborers for white landowners. These provisions, known as "Black Codes," denied blacks the right to lease or rent lands and levied them with a special capitation tax of one dollar annually. The edicts also required blacks to find employment and prevented them from "unlawfully assembling themselves together, either in the day or night." To do otherwise entailed the risk of arrest and being hired out by the state.[23]

The Mississippi Black Code included measures designed for children such as Missouri. If Missouri's parents refused to sign contracts and work, the state could take charge of the child without her parents' consent and make her the apprentice of someone of the state's choosing. Furthermore, the law directed that the child's former master would be first on the state's list as an acceptable mentor.[24]

Besides these severe economic limitations, Missouri and her parents would have had some real concerns about falling prey to the violence of whites who were frayed by the adjustments that Reconstruction forced upon them. The women of Missouri's family would have been particularly frightened about these racial flare-ups because they often involved horrifying sexual assaults. Such was the case in the Memphis Riot of 1866. Using a jostling incident between black militiamen and white policemen as pretext, an angry white mob attacked blacks throughout the city. Over the course of the three-day riots, forty-six black men, women, and children lost their lives, while several black churches, schools, and homes were burned to the ground. As part of their instruments of terror, white men savagely raped black women. During the federal investigation that followed the riot, several black women gave sworn testimony about their horrifying experiences. Frances Thompson described how seven white men entered the home where she lived with Lucy Smith, a sixteen-year-old black woman, and ordered the women to cook breakfast for them. After the intruders had eaten, they demanded sex from the women. When Thompson and Smith refused, the men beat and choked them and then drew their pistols, threatening to shoot the women and set the house on fire. Thompson and Smith submitted, and all seven men participated in the rape.[25]

Lucy Tibbs told an equally repugnant story of her experience during the riot. She explained how several men broke into her home, demanding to see her husband. When Tibbs informed them that he was away, the men threatened her and her two small children. Even though Tibbs was several months pregnant at the time, one of the men sexually assaulted her. While the rape was occurring, the other men plundered the house.[26]

African Americans living in Mississippi during Reconstruction also had fears of the Ku Klux Klan. Formed as a paramilitary organization to resist Reconstruction in Tennessee in 1866, the Klan bullied, intimidated, and murdered African Americans throughout the South in an effort to force their submission to Democratic rule.[27] The presence and activities of the Klan so frightened African Americans that many of them remembered their encounters for decades afterward. Lizzie Fant Brown, an ex-slave from Marshall County, Mississippi, recalled such an incident when she was a small child about the age of Missouri: "I was too little to remember the war but I remember seeing the KuKluxers. They came to the house one night and asked for water. I never see as much water passed out in my life, but they wasn't drinking it, they was just pouring it on the ground. They had on Injun rubber clothes so they wouldn't get wet. I don't know why they done that."[28]

Josephine Coxe, a former slave also from Marshall County, described the Klan and its acts of terror: "They would ride through niggers yards with their horses stamping and try to scare 'em by carrying a stick across the fence. They was mean to niggers over in Benton County. They would shoot 'em out of their houses and make 'em leave home. And when the niggers would sell their cotton in town and come home after dark, the Kluxers would stop 'em and take their money away from 'em."[29]

The onset of Radical Reconstruction expanded opportunities for former slaves such as Missouri's family. After blacks and their white Republican allies gained control of the state legislature in 1869, they quickly overturned the Mississippi Black Code. Now, blacks in the state could do as others across the South did and rent land as sharecroppers. Although still a marginal existence, sharecropping provided blacks with more family autonomy than they had working as gang laborers. With this greater independence, black men could better protect their wives and daughters from the sexual assaults of white male employers. Also, black families could exercise greater control over the roles of mothers and children within the black nuclear unit.[30]

Growing up as a black female in a family setting also meant that Missouri probably learned an assertiveness from her mother that her white counterparts would not have known. According to Jacqueline Jones, during Reconstruction whites often commented on the aggressive temperaments of black women, relative to black men, and how such attitudes defied traditional standards of submissiveness for women. Black women not only spoke out in ways that contradicted the status quo, but their dress further challenged convention. They often adorned themselves lavishly to illustrate both the legitimacy of their marital relationships and their newfound independence. This socialization would impact Missouri's future relationship with Isaac Bankston by making her more inclined to make demands of him.[31]

The 1880 census reveals that Missouri could read and write—a simple fact suggesting that she had probably received some formal education.[32] Such literacy would have instilled a great sense of pride in Missouri and her family.

To many black families of the era, acquiring education sig-
nified both the individual's and the community's evolution
from slavery to freedom.[33]

By 1880 Missouri had left her family's home and lived
and worked as a house servant for E. F. Miller, a prominent white businessman and plantation owner in Bolivar
County. She lived in a household with no fewer than sixteen
people, one of whom was her own six-month-old daughter.
The household was racially balanced, with nine people of
color and seven whites. It appears that most of the whites
held supervisory rolls or were skilled laborers. Only one
white household member seems to have been a menial laborer. On the other hand, blacks on the Miller plantation
were all laborers or worked as convict guards.[34]

Men greatly outnumbered women on the Miller plantation. Missouri was one of only two adult women listed on
the census rolls. The other woman, Nellie Ellis, was a forty-
year-old black woman who worked as a cook. No white
women lived on the Miller plantation. This likely meant
that Nellie and Missouri had to manage the entire domestic
operations of the Miller household.[35]

The 1880s witnessed the beginnings of the migration
of rural southerners to urban areas. Stimulated by the
growth of textile mills and declining opportunities on the
farm, many southerners saw the cities as places to find new
economic opportunity. Although a relatively small percent-
age of African Americans joined the migration movement
at this time, some blacks became wage earners in southern towns. Black women constituted a sizable proportion
of the migrants, serving as heads of households in 25 to 39
percent of all urban black families.[36]

Missouri moved to Arkansas City, Arkansas, sometime in 1881. Arkansas City was one of many towns experiencing significant growth in the early 1880s. Situated in the southeastern corner of Desha County beside the Mississippi River, Arkansas City was organized as a town on September 12, 1873. When the waters of the Mississippi eroded the port at Chicot City, Arkansas, movable facilities there were taken to Arkansas City and a new port constructed. The port would serve as a terminal for a new railroad line built by the Little Rock, Mississippi River and Texas Railway Company in 1880.[37] As a result of the port and railroad line, Arkansas City was transformed from a quiet town into one bustling with commercial activity. Its population around this time was 503 and growing. The town developed grocery stores such as Crawford and Bulloch and clothing and farm-supply enterprises such as Crenshaw. Establishments that specialized in liquor and tobacco and others that processed and sold meats also came to the town. In addition, advertisements for attorneys filled the local papers, along with solicitations by an assortment of medical practitioners.[38]

Arkansas City had other features that illustrated its up-and-coming status. Civic leaders boasted of the town's "capacious sidewalks" and the fact that the town had acquired an elevator and electric lights before other, better-known Arkansas towns such as Pine Bluff and Little Rock. The editors of the local paper, the *Arkansas City Journal,* referred to the town as the "Venice of Arkansas" and "a great and grand city" destined one day to "be second to none between St. Louis and New Orleans."[39]

Not all who visited Arkansas City during the early 1880s shared the unbridled enthusiasm of local leaders and boosters. While conducting an investigation of Arkansas "mounds"—probably Native American burial mounds—Edward Palmer, a visitor to the city, noted the "saloons" and "hard crowd." Palmer commented on the cockroaches at the hotel that crawled over the tables, walls, and floors, and he complained of the hotel's filthy and chilly rooms. Samuel Clemens, the famed American novelist better known as Mark Twain, also gave a description of Arkansas City that tempered assertions of the town's grandeur. He matter-of-factly wrote, "There are several rows and clusters of shabby houses, and a supply of mud sufficient to insure the town against famine in that article for a hundred years, for the overflow had but lately subsided. There were stagnant ponds in the streets, here and there and a dozen rude scows were scattered about lying aground wherever they happened to have been when the waters drained off and the people could do their visiting and shopping on foot once more."[40]

Despite Arkansas City's limitations, the potential of the town so impressed county residents that they voted overwhelmingly to make it the county seat in 1880. Isaac Bankston played a fairly conspicuous role in the process. As sheriff, he had the responsibility of gathering the election returns and reporting them to the county court. Shortly after the election, county officials voted to build a new courthouse in Arkansas City. The new courthouse would be very modern, adorned with a grand jury room, sheriff's office, jailer's house, and an iron jail cell. Isaac helped in the construction process by digging a well for the courthouse for $55.50.[41]

The relative modernity and economic opportunity in Arkansas City attracted Missouri to the town. Although undoubtedly forced to work in some service capacity, Missouri had come to a community where the sheer number of businesses and homes in need of laborers assured her of wages higher than what she received on the Miller plantation. Also, moving to the town placed her in closer proximity to larger numbers of blacks.[42]

At some point, chance apparently brought Missouri and Isaac together. On the surface, it would appear that their relationship had little hope of developing into anything lasting. Isaac was married, and southern society frowned on interracial intimacy that became public or formal. Yet, this pair refused to adhere to society's dictates. Eventually, Isaac and Missouri would make their way to a place southern society considered off-limits to a white man and a black woman: the marriage altar.

3

IN SEARCH OF
THEIR PLACE

When it came to interracial coupling, post–Civil War
Arkansas was much like the rest of the South. During the
antebellum period, black-white liaisons usually involved
white men and slave women. These affairs often operated beneath the public radar and, if known, were mostly
ignored and/or tolerated by the larger white society.[1] Few
white men spoke openly of their interracial associations or
openly acknowledged the biracial children they fathered.
In those instances when white men recognized mixed-
raced offspring, they usually did so in wills. Such was the
situation in *Campbell v. Campbell* (1845), an Arkansas case
in which the collateral heirs of the deceased Duncan G.
Campbell challenged his right to emancipate a slave girl
named Viney and leave her a five-thousand-dollar legacy.
In Campbell's final testament, he revealed that Viney was
his daughter by one of his slaves. Fortunately for Viney, the
Arkansas high court upheld Campbell's right to free her
and impart the inheritance.[2] In a similar Arkansas case,
Moss v. Sandefur (1847), evidence suggested that the deceased James H. Dunn, a white Hempstead County merchant, had intended to manumit Eliza, his daughter from

a slave woman named Mourning. However, Eliza would not receive her freedom because Dunn had not specified such a provision in his will.[3]

The tendency of white men to hide their coupling with black women stemmed to a large extent from the negative attitudes that whites had toward people of African descent. During the seventeenth century, Europeans began making much of racial differences and the supposed inferiority of nonwhite peoples, describing Africans, along with other people of color, as "brutish," "pagan," and "uncivilized." As part of this racial stereotyping, whites also gave sexualized labels to these groups. For Europeans, Africans were "savagely" sexual, with "hot and lascivious" carnal temperaments.[4]

As slavery took hold in the English colonies, the acceptance of stereotypes became more widespread. Consequently, white authorities developed a particular concern about interracial relationships. Along with regarding black-white coupling as repugnant to society, white leaders recognized two significant problems caused by such relationships. First, the children from interracial relationships blurred the lines of freedom in the colonies.[5] If blacks were by the very nature of their color presumed slaves and whites were regarded as free, what status would their biracial children have? Second, the colonial patriarchy worried about black men having access to white women. In colonies with sparse numbers of white women, white men feared that allowing interracial relationships to go unregulated jeopardized their own access to white women.[6]

To deal with these problems, many colonial assemblies instituted antimiscegenation laws that typically banned interracial marriage. Since whites could not legally marry blacks, whites could not fully convey their status on any children that came from sexual unions. In practice, because most sexual encounters occurred between white masters and slave women, antimiscegenation laws helped to ensure that most biracial children remained slaves. In those cases where black men and white women interacted sexually, other colonial legislation dictated that the offspring from these liaisons spend the first twenty years or more of their lives as servants.[7]

During the antebellum period, most southern states maintained their antimiscegenation statutes. By this time these provisions worked in conjunction with state adultery and fornication laws. Interracial couples who attempted to marry had their nuptials nullified by the state's antimiscegenation edict. The state then charged them with unlawful cohabitation, adultery, or fornication. Although technically these mandates applied to all interracial couples, state authorities used them mostly against interracial relationships involving free black men and white women. Such enforcement reveals the special privileges of white males in the antebellum South and the veritable powerlessness of white women. As long as white men sustained their interracial liaisons in relative secrecy, they had little to fear from legal authorities.[8]

After the Civil War, the onset of Radical Reconstruction raised questions about the legitimacy of state antimiscegenation laws. Not only did federal and state judges deliberate on the lawfulness of the edicts, but state judges also grappled with the constitutionality of antimiscegenation laws. As a result, the state supreme courts in Texas and

Alabama severely weakened or voided the statutes.[9] Other southern states—Louisiana, Mississippi, and Arkansas—either directly repealed the measures or omitted them from their civil codes.[10]

The abandonment of official efforts to punish interracial couples in these states made interracial relationships more conspicuous. This was especially true for Arkansas. On several occasions, the state's most widely read newspaper, the *Arkansas Gazette,* reported on interracial marriages, and census data from 1870 and 1880 reveals that numerous interracial couples had formalized their unions and established households together.[11]

The growing tendency of interracial couples to engage each other in a more public fashion did not mean that most people accepted these unions. To the contrary, throughout the Reconstruction period many southern whites worked to maintain antimiscegenation provisions and disparaged those who openly crossed the sexual color line. Also, southern whites came to associate the expansion of rights for African Americans with encouraging sexual unions between the races. As a white Arkansas delegate to the state's constitutional convention of 1868 bluntly put it, the "investing of an inferior race with social and political equality is the stepping stone to miscegenation."[12]

Although antimiscegenation laws lost ground in the South during Reconstruction, they never completely disappeared. In two states, Georgia and Tennessee, direct judicial challenges to antimiscegenation provisions failed to overturn them. In fact, the high courts in each case foreshadowed the judicial reasoning that would become commonplace once southern whites had regained local control.

In *Scott v. State* (1869) and *State v. Bell* (1872), the supreme courts of Georgia and Tennessee, respectively, upheld the sovereignty of states over the question of marriage and asserted that maintaining antimiscegenation laws was in society's best interest. For these courts, interracial relationships were "unnatural connections" that operated against "good morals" and produced "evil and evil only without any corresponding good." Furthermore, to these justices, African Americans constituted an "inferior race" that threatened only to "bring down" the superiority of whites if blacks were allowed to have legal unions with them.[13]

Ending Reconstruction brought the expansion of civil rights for African Americans to a halt. From state to state, southern whites structured constitutions and laws in ways that assured the political domination of whites. As part of this "redemption" process, southern states almost universally resurrected antimiscegenation laws. By 1880 only one Southern state, Louisiana, had failed to return the edicts to its civil code.[14]

When Missouri and Isaac began their relationship in 1881, they did so in an Arkansas and a South that was becoming far less tolerant of interracial coupling with each passing year. Missouri and Isaac surely knew of this increasing public disapproval. Also, they would have been aware of the reemerging legal obstacles to any formalized union between them. From state to state, authorities hauled interracial couples into court, convicting and sentencing them to years in prison for crossing the intimacy color line. Although most of these cases appear to have involved black men and white women, white male–black female unions sometimes felt the heavy hand of the southern judicial system.[15]

Knowing that their relationship was unlawful would certainly have made Missouri and Isaac more aware of the need to keep their interaction as inconspicuous as possible. Also, Isaac's marital status made secrecy an even greater imperative. The inevitable gossip that would arise should his relationship with Missouri become public knowledge likely had him doubly concerned. Not only would he fear the emotional distress that might befall his wife, Martha, but he also would know that his family's reputation was at stake. Provable revelations of infidelity could subject Martha and his children to ridicule and contempt. Fortunately for Isaac, Arkansas City was more than twenty miles away from his farm—a fact that probably made secrecy an easier matter than it might otherwise have been.[16]

Missouri, too, would have to keep the couple's relationship a secret. Generally, blacks frowned on adulterous affairs.[17] They were also often less than sympathetic to interracial coupling. In this regard, the saga of Isaac Hooper, a black farmer from Pulaski County, Arkansas, is especially revealing. According to the story, which was detailed in the *Arkansas Gazette,* Hooper had agreed to allow a white man named Stephens to board at his residence. However, after some time Hooper evicted Stephens because the white man sought to marry his daughter. Although the daughter seemed anxious to wed Stephens, Hooper refused to sanction the union. When Stephens attempted to abscond with the girl, Hooper chased him away with a sprouting hoe and threatened to shoot him. Eventually, Hooper solicited help from legal authorities in his effort to "keep a hungry white man away from marrying a nigger."[18]

Blacks opposed interracial marriage for a number of reasons. First, blacks were well aware of white hostility to such coupling. They knew not only that people who married across the color line ran the risk of being socially and economically ostracized by whites but also that such couples could become victims of white violence. Second, blacks recognized the illegality of interracial relationships and what that entailed: by denying authenticity to interracial marriages, antimiscegenation laws deprived spouses and biracial children of the privileges associated with legitimacy. Third, many African Americans disliked interracial marriage out of the fear that such unions threatened black racial solidarity. Potentially, mixed marriages offered the African Americans involved in such unions access to a white world that the black community at large could not enjoy. This was especially true for biracial children who, because of the lightness of their complexions, might eventually stop living as black people altogether to "pass" as white.[19]

To maintain secrecy, Missouri and Isaac likely exchanged their affections behind closed doors or in isolated places. They would have avoided any appearance of being a couple, especially in Arkansas City or in any other places where one or both of them would be known. Thus, while in Desha County towns, Missouri and Isaac would never have sat openly at a dinner table together. They would never have walked the streets holding hands or arm in arm. When they traveled together, which probably occurred only sparingly, they would ride by wagon with Isaac at the reins and Missouri in the back. Only when they thought they were clear of familiar people or passers-by would Missouri join Isaac on the seat of the wagon.[20]

Such methods of avoiding detection were common to interracial couples throughout the South. Most interracial lovers hid behind a veil of informality to deflect public scrutiny. As long as Missouri and Isaac avoided marrying each other or living together, their communities were likely to ignore their association. Even if authorities decided to invoke antimiscegenation laws against them, Missouri and Isaac could still escape punishment because they maintained separate households.[21]

Like other interracial couples seeking to evade public scrutiny, Missouri and Isaac could mask their relationship because they were similar in skin color. Although no photographs of the couple exist, people who encountered them outside of Desha County commented on the couple's closeness in skin color. When Missouri and Isaac secured a marriage license from the county clerk of Shelby County, Tennessee, the assistant clerk, J. E. Lewis, signed the document and put the word "colored" on the license.[22] This indicates that he believed Missouri and Isaac to be racially similar. Also, when J. E. Roberts, the black minister who presided over the nuptials, was asked why he performed the ceremony, he said that he thought Isaac was "a colored man" and went on to assert that Isaac had "a dark complexion."[23] And in the trial that followed public revelations of the marriage, Isaac defended himself against the charges of violating Tennessee's antimiscegenation law by claiming to be something other than white.[24] Since Missouri was recognizably mulatto, Isaac's dark complexion afforded the couple greater public freedom than they would have enjoyed otherwise.[25]

Missouri and Isaac entered into their affair observing certain unspoken rules that they obeyed for years. They knew the social and legal limitations and understood the risks. However, they eventually made the decision to defy convention and formally marry. Why? With the dearth of available evidence, no one can be exactly sure. Yet, there are clues from Isaac's personal behavior, Missouri's economic condition, and the couple's particular circumstances that offer some insight into why they moved their liaison from a secret courtship to a formal marriage.

One factor that possibly influenced Isaac's thinking was his willingness, as discussed in the previous chapter, to align with blacks politically and economically. Although such relationships do not suggest that Isaac viewed blacks as equals, they reveal that to some extent he felt that associating with African Americans served his needs and desires. His de facto dependence on blacks necessitated a regular interaction with them and thus bettered the chances that he would develop some degree of affection for Missouri.

Missouri's willingness to push the parameters of her relationship with Isaac to the point of marriage may have stemmed from her desire for greater financial security. Southern society severely limited the occupational choices of black women in the late nineteenth century. According to Tera Hunter, more than 90 percent of black wage-earning women worked in a domestic capacity. Domestic workers normally labored every day of the week, toiling ten to twelve hours daily. Despite the long hours and hard work, black women earned no more than one to two dollars weekly. This sparse compensation, coupled with the lack of occupational choices, left many black women economically marginalized.[26] In Missouri's mind, an informal sex-for-security relationship may have lacked the perceived freedom from financial worry that a marriage could bestow. In part, then, Missouri may have sought marriage to Isaac in hopes of bettering her economic condition.

Another factor that undoubtedly had an impact on Missouri and Isaac's relationship was the birth of a child.[27] There is no record of the date of birth, but it seems that the couple had a son in 1881 or 1882. The child became public knowledge when newspaper coverage of their relationship appeared in 1884. Although Missouri had become a mother before moving to Arkansas from Mississippi, the daughter recorded in the 1880 census does not appear to be the same child mentioned in later reports of Missouri's involvement with Isaac; that child was identified as a small boy. It is possible that Missouri left her daughter with others before her relocation to Arkansas or that the child died shortly after the census was taken.[28]

The birth of a child could well have made Isaac feel a greater sense of responsibility for Missouri. When children became part of an interracial relationship, some southern white men came to regard the women of color and their biracial children as part of their family and treated them accordingly. For example, during the 1840s, A. H. Foster, a white slave owner in Louisiana, fathered several children by a slave woman named Leah; he then moved the entire family to Cincinnati, Ohio, where he freed them and set them up in a home. Foster did not live with Leah and her children while they were in Ohio, but he gave them financial support for more than four years. In 1852, after apparently growing tired of this long-distance arrangement, Foster took Leah and their offspring with him to Texas, where they lived together until his death in 1867.[29]

In another instance, which occurred in Mississippi in 1868, a white man named H. W. Kinard began living with a woman of color. The couple had three children over a ten-year period together. Instead of denying his paternity, Kinard openly caressed and coddled his children. Neighbors also observed the family lying together in the same bed. The state would later use this evidence of genuine affection for his family against Kinard, convicting him of unlawful cohabitation.[30]

In all probability, the fact of a child had a profound affect on Missouri's own attitude toward her relationship with Isaac. With an additional mouth to feed, she would have been even more concerned about financial security. Also, she likely had concerns about the negative labels society attached to children born out of wedlock. Like other blacks, Missouri wanted to raise her child in a married household.[31]

There is at least one other reason why Missouri and Isaac may have decided to formalize their relationship: they might have simply fallen in love with each other. For historians, making conjectures about love is often difficult. Without extant letters or other recorded statements declaring love as a motivation, historians generally feel more comfortable tying individual decisions to social, political, or economic factors. Love often defies what generally constitutes reasonable and logical thinking. It does not necessarily arise within the strict confines of a community's value structure. Furthermore, because human beings are complicated, the emotion of love may involve personal compromises and mixed feelings that make it hard for the historian to analyze. Yet, it is still possible that Missouri and Isaac's relationship led to marriage at least in part because of those personal, intimate, and less obvious attractions that subtly nurture relationships. Despite the strong societal opposition, for Missouri and Isaac the decision to marry may have been a natural expression of a passionate, heartfelt adoration that they had long held for each other.

* * *

Prior to leaving for Memphis, where he and Missouri would marry, Isaac became heavily involved in a case that attracted statewide attention. Alfred Werner, a white planter under contract with Desha County to use convicts as laborers, was indicted for his alleged involvement in the death of William Sharp, a poor white transient from Illinois. According to state prosecutors, Werner had ordered the beating of Sharp by black convict guards because of Sharp's refusal to plough and do other forms of farm work. Sharp had been arrested by Constable George Hundley in Red Fork Township for failing to pay a two-dollar boarding fee. Joseph H. Jones, the justice of the peace in Red Fork, imposed a ten-dollar penalty upon Sharp— a fine he was also unable to pay. Jones remanded him to Hundley, who in turn delivered him to Werner in accordance with the county policy that had been established by Sheriff Isaac Bankston.[32]

Werner took possession of Sharp on July 16, 1883, and Sharp died the next day. Werner immediately ordered the burial of Sharp's body without giving notice to any coroner or justice of the peace. State authorities arrested Werner on July 18, after being tipped off by some of the black farm guards who had not participated in the beatings. Officials then exhumed Sharp's body and convened a grand jury that indicted Werner and three of his black labor guards, Albert Bess, Dean Freeman, and Herman Johnson. The grand jury committed the men to the jail in Arkansas City to await trial. As Werner and the guards were being transported to the jail by boat, an incident occurred. An angry mob followed the boat as far as it could, shouting profanity and making angry gestures toward the accused men. One person in the crowd fired a shot that struck Werner in the hip. Though seriously wounded, Werner survived.[33]

While Werner was recovering in the Arkansas City jail, B. F. Merritt, the Desha county judge, granted Werner bail in the sum of ten thousand dollars, perhaps in an attempt to keep him from further harm. Isaac then transported Werner to Memphis, Tennessee, to give him an opportunity to make his bond. There, Werner presented Isaac a bond signed by two men, W. C. Werner and E. C. Roseberry, who agreed to be securities for Werner's promise to appear in court on the day of his trial. Isaac accepted the bond and took Werner back across the Mississippi River to Crittenden County, Arkansas, where Werner was released.[34]

When word of the release became public, some citizens of Desha County called a mass meeting to discuss the bail and the bond. The result was a resolution signed by civic leaders, including former county judge W. C. Peterson, that condemned the actions of Isaac and Judge Merritt. The declaration called the bail set by Merritt "reprehensible" and expressed outrage at Isaac's willingness to accept a "pretended security" that was "in utter defiance of the ends of justice."[35]

Despite the fears of petitioners that Werner might flee, the accused man did appear in court. The proceedings were held in Pine Bluff, Arkansas, after the defense successfully requested a change of venue. At trial, prosecutors painted a picture of gross brutality on Werner's part. According to state witnesses, Werner had called Sharp a "damned Yankee tramp" and ordered some of the guards to strip Sharp and hold him down while other guards ruthlessly beat him. Eyewitnesses to the flogging recalled that Werner gave Sharp "fifty licks." Allegedly, Sharp cried out, "Mr. Werner, please have pity on a poor white man." Werner mandated five more lashes and then placed Sharp in a jail cell, where he died shortly thereafter.[36]

In his defense, Werner denied ordering the whippings, claiming that the convict guards had acted alone without his knowledge. His attorneys also raised questions about the credibility of the state's witnesses, reminding the jury that most of them were convicts on the Werner farm. Despite the defense's best efforts, the Pine Bluff jury saw little validity in its arguments and found Werner guilty of murder. Werner was sentenced to twenty-one years in the state penitentiary. Though the scope of Isaac's involvement in the trial is unknown, it is certain that he attended and participated in the proceedings, probably serving as a defense witness and answering questions about the county's convict-lease policy and Werner's conduct with regard to laborers.[37]

The trial ended on December 22, 1883. According to newspaper reports that would appear some weeks later, after Isaac's relationship with Missouri became public, Isaac "threw up everything" immediately following the Werner trial and dashed back to Arkansas City to see Missouri. James S. Ross, a resident of Arkansas City and Isaac's deputy, told reporters that Isaac had been acting "strangely" for some time and that he had been forced to "manage the affairs" of the sheriff's office. In fact, Ross had became so disgusted with Isaac's behavior that he resigned his post as deputy.[38] During the last week in December 1883, Missouri and Isaac absconded to Memphis.[39] While it cannot said for certain that the controversy surrounding the Werner trial had a direct bearing on Isaac's decision to run off to Memphis with Missouri, it does seem possible that it contributed to his troubled state of mind and hardened his resolve to start a new life elsewhere.

It would take a few days for Missouri, Isaac, and their small son to trek from Arkansas City to Memphis. In making this journey, Isaac was leaving behind a white family—Martha, Isaac Jr., and Laura—and a town that may well have become increasingly suspicious of his relationship with Missouri. He was headed for a place where he and Missouri hoped they could live in obscurity together and raise their child. Yet, despite the more than one hundred miles that separated Memphis from Desha County, the busy Tennessee city proved to be too close to home.

4

FROM MEMPHIS TO MARRIAGE AND MISERY

In late December 1883, when Missouri and Isaac arrived in the city, Memphis bustled with activity. Seven railroad lines connected the Bluff City to other areas throughout the South and Midwest, while the Memphis City Rail conjoined the city's ten wards. Steamboats bellowed their daily entries and exits in the river port. Some of them exported cotton, while others brought in passengers of prestige who often lodged at one of the city's three luxury hotels, the Peabody, Gaston, or New Clarendon. Businesses dotted the city landscape. Main Street housed a number of these enterprises, including clothing stores such as Buxbaum, Lemmon & Gale, and Johnson & Vance; jewelers such as C. L. Byrd & Company and James S. Welkins; and banks such as the Memphis Building and Savings Association. The metropolis also boasted a theater, skating rink, fairgrounds, and a number of other parks and recreational facilities.[1]

It was an exciting place. The *Memphis Daily Appeal,* one of the city's nine newspapers, highlighted the myriad of occurrences. The Leubrie Theatre showcased nationally acclaimed plays such as the *Pearl of Savoy* and *Fanchon.* Baseball games and boxing matches were the norm.

Expositions also made their way to the city. One that attracted considerable attention came in May 1884, when Memphis hosted a race between a horseman and a bicycle rider.[2]

Even medicine manufacturers tapped into this "everything is possible" atmosphere in Memphis by advertising products that claimed to cure a host of maladies. The makers of "Ayer's Sarsaparilla" alleged that it purified "blood corrupted by disease," a condition it warned that if left untreated could be passed on to offspring. Another Ayers medicine, "Cherry Pectoral," was touted as a counteractant to bronchitis, laryngitis, and even acute pneumonia. For women, "Hagan's Magnolia Balm" supposedly alleviated "sallowness, redness, pimples, and blotches and all diseases and imperfections of the skin," while "Samarian Nervine" healed female-specific nervous conditions.[3]

The city's liveliness was one of the factors that attracted Missouri and Isaac. Another was its proximity to Arkansas City. Memphis was close enough for a horseback journey of less than a week's duration, yet far enough away to lessen the possibility of running into anyone either of them knew. The city's large and diverse population was another plus. In 1884 Memphis had no fewer than fifty-five thousand people living in and around the city, of which approximately twenty thousand were of African descent.[4] Here, Missouri and Isaac hoped to achieve an inconspicuousness that would allow them greater freedom.

The size, strength, and history of the black community would have been particularly alluring to Missouri. Prior to the Civil War, very few blacks resided in the city. In 1860 only thirty-nine hundred African Americans lived in Memphis, as opposed to more than nineteen thousand whites. These demographics during the antebellum period were typical of most southern cities with regard to the numbers of African Americans. As the importance of cotton grew and the numbers of white newcomers increased in southern cities, masters removed black slaves to the rural areas in order to increase cotton production profits.[5]

After Memphis fell to Union troops on June 6, 1862, runaway slaves from nearby areas came to the city in droves, seeing Memphis as a refuge in their quest for freedom. Although initially greeted by a less-than-welcoming Union army that designated them as "contraband," put them to work without wages, and allowed masters the right to reclaim them, the ever-increasing numbers of escaped slaves eventually forced military leaders to adjust their policy. Before the end of the year, Union officers had organized former slaves into camps and began leasing them to loyal planters who promised to provide them with room, board, and wages.[6]

The Emancipation Proclamation further increased the numbers of blacks who relocated to Memphis. By the spring of 1863, blacks were joining the Union army. The recruitment of blacks affected Memphis's population because the city served as both a recruiting station and base of operations for many black units. When black men enlisted in the Union army, they often brought their wives and children to live in Memphis with them.[7]

By the war's end, more than sixteen thousand blacks inhabited Memphis. Although this number somewhat declined in the 1870s, the black population more than doubled in the two decades that followed. By 1900 no other southern urban area could claim a more substantial black growth rate than the Bluff City.[8]

Memphis's black community began Reconstruction in an atmosphere of growing intolerance. By the end of the war, local whites complained about blacks forgetting their proper station and presuming to act as social equals. The large number of Irish laborers in the city registered particularly strong opposition to local blacks, viewing them as competitors for unskilled jobs. When the army began mustering out black soldiers, these men joined the swelling ranks of unskilled laborers. The larger those numbers became, the greater the enmity between whites and blacks of the laboring class. This volatile situation exploded on May 1, 1866, when the mostly Irish police force and fire departments attacked blacks throughout the city. After three days of violence, forty-eight persons were dead: forty-six blacks and two whites. Roughly one hundred blacks had been robbed by looters, and five black women had been raped. Also, the Irish destroyed every black church and school in the city.[9]

Blacks in Memphis rebuilt their community after the riot, reconstructing their churches and schools, mostly through self-help.[10] By the time Missouri and Isaac arrived in the city in late 1883, black Memphians had eight schools from which to choose, as well as no fewer than thirty churches.[11] Over the course of the 1870s and 1880s, blacks also used their newly acquired voting rights to affect the power structure of the city. Although blacks never dominated Memphis politics during this period, between 1872 and 1879 blacks won 19 out of a total of 160 contests for seats on the Board of Common Councilmen, the lower house of the city's bicameral General Council. Moreover, blacks gained a presence on both the police and fire forces.[12]

The three major yellow fever epidemics that beset Memphis during the 1870s played an important and interesting role in the expansion of opportunities for local blacks as policemen. During the epidemics, over twenty-five thousand people contracted yellow fever, with more than seven thousand losing their lives. Thousands fled the city out of fear. The Memphis population declined during the decade from forty thousand to thirty-four thousand, with whites losing far greater numbers to the disease and subsequent flight than blacks, who generally had a stronger immunity to the disease. Memphis policemen, required by their duties to come into close contact with the infected, suffered particularly severe manpower losses. The decline in the number of white policemen, the desire of city leaders to maintain order, and the agitation of the black community forced civic leaders to do what they had previously been unwilling to do: hire black policemen. By 1878 black policemen patrolled the streets of Memphis for the first time in the city's history. Even after the epidemics ended, blacks continued serving on the police force, constituting one-fourth of its numbers in 1882 and 1884.[13]

Although the yellow fever epidemics helped blacks establish a place for themselves on the Memphis Police Department, the crisis served in the long term to dilute black power in city politics. In response to the devastation and dislocation produced by the pandemic, the Tennessee General Assembly rescinded the city's charter and created a new governmental structure. The General Council was replaced by a bicameral legislative council whose members were elected at large instead of by wards. When Memphis blacks had been successful in the past in winning seats on the General Council, it had usually occurred in wards where blacks were in the majority. With the city-wide election system in place, only one African American would secure a seat on the Legislative Council in the 1880s.[14]

Despite their declining political fortunes in the 1880s, Memphis blacks still maintained a thriving community. Black churches could be found in nearly every ward of the city.[15] These institutions provided blacks with more than religious instruction; they also sponsored mutual relief, educational, and burial societies and funded private schools. Local African Americans operated and attended LeMoyne Normal Institute, the first black institution of higher learning in the city.[16] LeMoyne students learned not only advanced reading and writing but also a number of vocational skills.[17] Blacks in the city owned more than one hundred businesses, which included drayage operations (drays were two-wheeled horse- or mule-drawn carts that hauled cotton), hack services (transportation companies that used four-wheeled carriages pulled by one or two horses to carry passengers to in-town destinations), saloons, barbershops, restaurants, hotels, and boarding houses. Also, black Memphians worked in a variety of occupations, even pursuing professional careers as bankers, brokers, clerks, bookkeepers, teachers, and lawyers.[18]

Although the social atmosphere in Memphis allowed blacks to achieve some economic success, they increasingly had to deal with segregation and other exclusionary practices. In some instances such as with churches, blacks chose to segregate themselves, preferring to control their own institutions. At other times, however, exclusionary policies were forced on them, particularly in the use of city services. For example, in March 1881 Memphis policemen forcefully arrested Julia Hooks, a young black pianist and teacher, for refusing to give up a seat reserved for whites on the main floor of a Memphis theater. In the ensuing trial before a local judge, Hooks and other black witnesses testified that they had occupied seats on the main floor in the past without interference. The theater manager confirmed their statements but cited a recently instituted policy that required blacks to sit in a "colored balcony" when the facility was crowded. The judge fined Hooks five dollars.[19]

In a similar case in May 1884, Ida B. Wells, a young school teacher, purchased a seat in the ladies' coach of a train. She initially thought nothing of her actions as it was her usual practice to ride in the ladies' coach. When the conductor collecting tickets informed Wells that she could not ride in the first-class car, she protested and refused to move. The conductor attempted to pull Wells out of her seat, but she fought back, biting the back of the conductor's hand. Unsuccessful in displacing Wells, the conductor enlisted the help of two other men, who assisted him in dragging Wells to the smoking car, a place reserved for second-class passengers. At this point, Wells chose to leave the train rather than acquiesce to the conductor's actions.[20]

Wells sued the railroad company for damages, securing the legal services of James Greer, a local white attorney and former criminal court judge. Winning the case, Wells was awarded five hundred dollars. However, the railroad appealed the ruling to the Tennessee Supreme Court, citing their right to segregate blacks by dint of the recent U.S. Supreme Court decision in the Civil Rights Cases of 1883. In reviewing those cases, the nation's highest court had declared unconstitutional the Civil Rights Act of 1875, a law mandating equal access to public facilities. The Tennessee Supreme Court sided with the company and reversed the lower-court ruling.[21]

Blacks not only had to endure forced segregation in Memphis but also had to face a hostile white press. A review of the *Memphis Daily Appeal* during the few months that Missouri and Isaac lived in the city illustrates this acrimony against the black community. Rarely did any positive coverage of blacks appear in the paper. When such articles did occur, they were usually like the one that praised the LeMoyne Institute for teaching black students skills that would keep them in service capacities useful to whites. Indeed, the paper lauded the school's leaders for teaching girls "needlework, and housekeeping" and instructing boys in "carpentry and the general use of tools." According to the article, the work at the school "merits and should receive the sympathy and support of every good citizen."[22]

More often than not, articles appearing in the *Memphis Daily Appeal* depicted blacks as buffoons or criminals, when it noticed them at all. For example, on March 13, 1884, in a section titled "Local Paragraphs," the paper mentioned blacks twice. In the first instance, the *Appeal* referred to Jerry Jones, a black man, as a "darky" and told of how he went to the county clerk's office with fifty cents determined to buy a marriage license, only to be "struck to his knees" upon learning that $2.50 was required. According to the paper, Jones begged in town all day until he acquired the desired amount. Just beneath the Jones story was a one-line item about Abe Temple, a black man who was put on trial for bastardy. Almost daily, readers found stories portraying blacks as mentally incompetent or criminally inclined. Such demeaning coverage revealed the undertone of racial antipathy and disregard that most whites had toward blacks in the city.[23]

The intensifying public signs of racial tension and black exclusion were hardly unique to Memphis. During this period, many southern cities saw the growth of de facto segregation. According to Howard Rabinowitz, the segregation practices of whites in southern cities prior to 1890 presaged the coming of de jure segregation. By the 1890s Jim Crow laws would become fixtures in the American South, signifying and enforcing a formal white-over-black power structure.[24]

Memphis, though hardly a paragon of racial enlightenment, had what Missouri and Isaac needed: reasonable distance; a dense, diverse population; and a well-developed African American community. It seemed to be a relatively safe haven for interracial couples. In fact, Missouri and Isaac were not the only interracial couple from Arkansas to view the city in this way. On November 6, 1883, the *Arkansas Gazette* carried the first of three articles about L. G. Pollard, a prominent white minister of the Methodist Episcopal Church, and Eliza Dillahey, a sixteen-year-old woman of color. According to the *Gazette,* Pollard was a long-time resident of Arkansas from a distinguished family. After joining the ministry as a young man, he eventually became head elder of the Methodist Episcopal Church in the Little Rock

District. His first wife died of tuberculosis, leaving him the sole parent of a young boy. Pollard married a second time but obtained a divorce about six weeks before marrying Dillahey. In the divorce decree, Pollard claimed that he and his second wife were going their separate ways because of "incompatible temperaments." However, it was later revealed that Pollard's second wife left him after learning of his affection for Dillahey.[25]

The Pollard-Dillahey marriage grabbed the paper's attention for more than just its interracial nature. Apparently, Pollard was also guilty of forging a parental consent form. When Dillahey's mother was asked if she had agreed to the nuptials, she denied having signed anything. Yet, Pollard and the black minister who presided over the wedding, W. H. Higgins, presented one when securing the marriage license. Higgins's signature was also on the consent form as a witness. Believing the document to be authentic and Dillahey to be a white woman, the Pulaski county clerk issued the license. After the marriage, Pollard and Dillahey did not stay in Little Rock but left for Memphis by train.[26]

* * *

When Missouri and Isaac arrived in the city, they took lodging with their small child at a boarding house owned by Cornelia Winston, a forty-year-old mulatto woman.[27] The 1880 census showed that Winston, like Missouri, had been born in Mississippi. Also, Winston was herself the product of an interracial union. Her father had been born in England and her mother in North Carolina.[28]

While staying at the Winston place, Missouri had a chance encounter with J. E. Roberts, an African Methodist Episcopal minister. Roberts and his wife, Hattie, were also boarding at the Winston home while making their way from their former residence in LaGrange, Missouri, to their new home in Cotton Plant, Arkansas. The *Arkansas Gazette* described Minister Roberts as "an intelligent looking colored man, almost a mulatto" and Hattie as a "quite handsome mulatto."[29] Somewhere in the home, a conversation transpired between Minister Roberts and Missouri in which Roberts asked Missouri about her relationship with Isaac. Ashamed of having to admit that she had borne a son out of wedlock, Missouri initially told the minister that she had been married to Isaac for three years—a story she recanted just a few moments later. She went on to tell Roberts that she and Isaac had been "living" together for three years and that Isaac had repeatedly promised they would marry as soon as they located a minister. Missouri expressed frustration with Isaac's failure to carry through on his promise, saying that "she could stand it no longer."[30]

While Missouri and the Roberts were conversing, Isaac entered the room. Upon meeting Isaac for the first time, Roberts later recalled, he believed that Missouri and Isaac shared similar racial heritages. He said that Isaac had a "dark complexion" and looked like "a colored man."[31]

Within two days after meeting Roberts, Missouri, Isaac, and their son left the Winston place and rented a house on Rayburn Avenue just below South Street. While at the new residence, Missouri and Isaac discussed their conversation with Roberts and decided to accept his offer to perform a wedding ceremony. Although Isaac had put Missouri off about marriage before, this time he did not hesitate. Shortly thereafter, Missouri and Isaac conveyed their intentions to Roberts, and on December 29, 1883, the three of them made their way to the county clerk's office to secure a marriage license. It had been just a week since Missouri and Isaac had left Arkansas.

The county clerk's office was headed by Hugh B. Cullen, a Virginia native, who had moved to Memphis in 1871. Cullen worked as a real estate agent early in his career and over time built an agency so lucrative and well known that it gained him a place in the prestigious Memphis Cotton Exchange publication, *Memphis As She Is: Rambles in the Path of Industrial and Commercial Circles.* Not only was Cullen a successful businessman, but he also had a strong civic reputation as a member of two reputed organizations: the Knights Templars of Masonry and the Encampment of Odd-Fellows. He married Lizzie Gibbs, a Memphis native, in 1873, and the couple had five children. After serving several years as a deputy county clerk, Cullen won an election to the top position in 1882.[32]

Cullen had two deputy clerks, Lewis Kettman and James E. Lewis, a twenty-seven-year-old retail grocer.[33] It was James Lewis who actually dealt with Missouri, Isaac, and Roberts when they came for the license; his name accompanies that of Cullen in two places on the document.[34] To marry in Tennessee, as was true in most southern states, the groom had to sign a bond for a fixed sum of money, assuring the state that he was eligible to marry. By law, the groom could only sign the bond if he was not underage, already married to someone else, or ineligible because of close blood relationship or racial difference. The amount of the bonds differed from state to state. In Tennessee at that time, the amount was $1,250. No money actually changed hands. The bond acted as a promise to pay and usually was backed by a friend or relative commonly known as a bondsman. Should the clerk ever find reason to sue the groom for violating the bond agreement, the bondsman would have to pay any legal damages if the groom defaulted.[35]

Roberts served as the bondsman for Missouri and Isaac. The couple paid a small fee of $2.50 for the license, which had "colored" marked on it.[36] Like Roberts, Lewis thought that both Missouri and Isaac were African Americans. Thus, on two separate occasions involving different people, Isaac had been identified as a man of color. This suggests that Isaac had features—dark complexion, hair, maybe even the structure of his nose and lips—that signaled to others that he was nonwhite. The perceptions of both Roberts and Lewis assume even greater significance when one considers that both men faced potential legal action for misjudging an individual's race. Ministers who married interracial couples could be fined up to five hundred dollars. The county clerk (presumably deputy clerks as well) could be sued by any private citizen and also fined five hundred dollars for knowingly issuing licenses to persons forbidden by law to marry.[37] Because of these legal dangers, Roberts and Lewis must have believed that Missouri and Isaac were part of the same racial group.

After getting the license, Missouri and Isaac were married later that day. It is likely that at least the couple's child and Hattie Roberts were in attendance. One can only speculate about what crossed through the minds of the couple as they listened to the minister's words. Missouri likely felt a mixture of joy and relief. In her mind, she was finally gaining the legitimacy for herself and her child that she had

long desired. As for Isaac, he probably relished the fact that
Missouri had been appeased, but his thoughts must also
have gone back to the wife, family, and life that he had left
behind in Desha County. What if his marriage to Missouri
became known? How could he navigate the troubled waters of such a revelation? By the end of the ceremony, Isaac
probably had made two promises—one orally to Missouri
and one silently to himself. To Missouri, Isaac vowed to forsake all others, but to himself Isaac swore to keep all others
from learning the truth.

However, at the very moment Missouri and Isaac stood
before Roberts, Isaac's determination to keep his marriage
to Missouri out of the public eye had already been compromised. The *Memphis Daily Appeal* routinely listed marriage
licenses that had been obtained, and on the following day,
Saturday, December 30, 1883, the paper duly reported on
the issuance of Missouri and Isaac's license.[38] In the context of the abundant news recorded on that day, the listing
of the license was a tiny matter. Its impact upon Missouri
and Isaac's fortunes would be massive, however. Ten days
later, the first of several articles specifically about the marriage of Missouri and Isaac appeared in Arkansas papers.
On Tuesday, January 9, 1884, the *Arkansas Gazette* reported
that Isaac had failed to "make his official bond as sheriff
of Desha County" and that the office had become vacated.
The article then mentioned that the recent report of Isaac's
"marriage to a colored woman" and his "failure to return to
explain the matter" were the reasons for his failure to give
the bond.[39]

The *Arkansas Democrat* published a similar story the
next day, noting that the "sureties on the bond of Sheriff
Isaac Bankston" had asked a circuit court to relieve them

of responsibility for the bond. They cited Isaac's absence and the allegations of his marriage to a "negro woman" in Memphis. The circuit court freed the sureties of responsibility and ordered Isaac to file another bond by January 7, 1884, a deadline he had already missed. The paper went on to offer what read very much like an obituary: "Bankston has served several terms as Sheriff of the county, and until recently was considered a faithful and reliable official. He leaves a wife and several children, whom if reports are true, he has forsaken for a strange colored woman."[40]

January 10, 1884, was also a day when the *Arkansas Gazette* published a follow-up article about the alleged marriage. It reiterated the problem of the bond and mentioned Isaac's failure to make the revised target date. Further, the paper offered the first comments about Missouri that went beyond her being identified as "colored." A single sentence noted that she had been a former resident of Arkansas City and was "there known to bear a bad character."[41]

On January 11, in the last of the first wave of accounts about Missouri and Isaac's marriage, the *Gazette* printed a story declaring that Isaac was "wrong in his head." The article explained what it called Isaac's "strange actions" prior to his absconding to Memphis with Missouri, and it once again offered some description of her. This time it labeled Missouri "a somewhat fascinating woman, not particularly handsome, but of some pleasing address." The article also subtly suggested that she possessed some mystical powers that she used to exercise "a strange influence over the erring sheriff."[42]

The characterization of Missouri and Isaac's actions by the press was predictable. The news media saw their marriage as irrational and reprehensible. The brief description of Missouri fit into the perceptions that whites held of black women. Whites viewed black women as inherently promiscuous and beguiling. To say that Missouri had a "bad character" surprised few of the paper's white readers and reinforced stereotypes of black women as Jezebels. Conversely, Isaac was portrayed as acting out of character. White society did not want to believe that a person once held in such high esteem could so grossly violate community norms by expressing genuine affection for a member of so degraded a race. Something must have taken control of Isaac's reason, the paper suggested. Missouri, the mulatto seductress, must have led him astray.[43]

By the first week of February 1884, Isaac was back at his home in Desha County. There is no way of knowing whether Isaac discovered prior to his return that news of his marriage to Missouri had preceded him. Almost a month had passed since the first reports.[44] However, when confronted with the allegations of his marriage to Missouri, Isaac reacted with shock, disbelief, and anger. He was shocked that the news of the marriage had become public. Dumbfounded that his once-solid reputation had suffered such a damaging blow, he was angry that newspapers throughout the state had so energetically disseminated the story. Because of the excitement and curiosity generated by the charges, Isaac felt compelled to deny Missouri many times to friends and reporters.[45]

Queried about traveling to Memphis with Missouri and what accounted for his lengthy absence, Isaac responded with a contrived answer. He acknowledged that he had indeed taken "the colored woman" to Memphis but had done so only as part of his duties as sheriff. Isaac hinted that Missouri had gotten into some trouble and that he had transported her out of Arkansas City to ensure her safety. Isaac became so embroiled in his own mendacity—and so determined to restore his public luster—that he even threatened the offending newspapers with libel suits. This bluff proved to be a strategic blunder because it led reporters to seek supporting evidence for what really happened.[46]

Within a week of Isaac's announcement about possible libel suits against the newspapers, the *Arkansas Gazette* published an interview with Minister Roberts about the Bankston affair. Not only did Roberts attest to the fact of the marriage, but he also described in gripping detail the primary role that Isaac had played in the whole saga. The minister's account revealed that Isaac had not fallen under the spell of a witchlike colored woman. Instead, the former sheriff had engaged in a secret life with Missouri for years—one that had produced a child. Roberts told the press that Isaac had made repeated promises of marriage to Missouri and, far worse, that Isaac had allowed Roberts to believe that he was a man of color.[47]

The news of Isaac's deception spread. On February 14, 1884, the Shelby County Clerk's Office sent Roberts a letter demanding that he return the marriage license.[48] In response, Roberts explained that he had given the license to Isaac with instructions to have it recorded. Fearing legal liabilities, Roberts swore out an affidavit about his role in Missouri and Isaac's marriage shortly after receiving the clerk's letter.[49]

Even if Cullen's office had been inclined to ignore reports of Missouri and Isaac's unlawful marriage, the timing of events made that a virtual impossibility. That same month, Cullen was sued by George Elliot, the attorney for James Chambers and Nannie Bennett, for unlawfully issuing them a marriage license. Chambers and Bennett were an interracial couple who had secured a license on July 10, 1883, from the clerk's office. As noted above, state law allowed any citizen to recover damages from a county clerk who "willfully and knowingly" issued a marriage license to persons forbidden to marry each other. According to Elliot, on July 10, 1883, Chambers and Bennett sent John Bridges to apply for a marriage license for them. With Bridges, a black man, acting as bondsman, the clerk issued the document, marking it "colored." After the wedding, James Lee, the black minister who had performed the ceremony, returned the license. Chambers, a white railroad laborer, and Bennett, a woman of color, lived together as husband and wife in South Memphis in a small cabin for several months. Despite neighbors' complaints, law enforcement officials took no action against the couple until February 16, 1884, when Deputy Sheriff A. K. Hancock showed up with a warrant for their arrest. Kicking open their locked door, Hancock found Chambers and Bennett in bed together with their six-week-old infant. Hancock took the family into custody. That same day, Elliot initiated the suit, claiming that the real fault lay with Cullen and his office for issuing the license. Although the clerk's office would subsequently be cleared of any wrongdoing, the negative publicity made Cullen and his deputies particularly sensitive about enforcing the law. When Missouri and Isaac's affair came to their attention, there was little chance that the clerk's office would be inclined to let the matter pass.[50]

His word against that of a colored minister—that was how Isaac probably phrased his denials of marriage to Missouri. Isaac was no doubt well aware of whites' skepticism toward the claims of blacks whenever their accounts of events clashed with those of whites. Some of Isaac's Arkansas City neighbors probably even maintained confidence in him despite the growing evidence to the contrary. However, at least one neighbor, James Coates, a white attorney and resident of Arkansas City, believed otherwise. Coates was a divorcé who lived alone. His former wife, Mary Coates, worked as a storekeeper and lived in McConnell Township in neighboring Chicot County with the couple's three children, Albert, John, and Mary. Coates had marginal success as an attorney. He placed no ads in the *Arkansas City Journal* nor held elected office. His name is absent among those of the prominent men of the county in *Goodspeed's Biographical and Historical Memoirs of Southern Arkansas.* Yet, for reasons that can only be guessed at, Coates would play a pivotal role in the subsequent legal effort to punish Missouri and Isaac.

On March 6, 1884, three days after the return of Missouri and Isaac's marriage license, the district attorney general for Shelby County, General G. P. M. Turner, convened a grand jury to review the facts in the case. The state sought an indictment against the couple on the charge of "illegal cohabitation." The grand jury called four witnesses: Minister J. E. Roberts, Hattie Roberts, James D. Coates, and Abe Manley, a local blacksmith. Coates acted as both witness and special prosecutor—his surprising role in the latter capacity owing to an unusual set of circumstances that will be explained more fully later. By the end of the day, the state had its indictment. Missouri and Isaac had been formally charged.[51]

Despite the grand jury's actions in early March, Isaac was not arrested until May 5, 1884. James Ross, though he had earlier resigned as Isaac's deputy, had been made acting sheriff of Desha County, and it was he who apprehended his former superior and placed him in the county jail. Isaac was to be held until Captain George T. O'Haver, a six-year veteran of the Memphis police force, could arrive with extradition papers. The city dispatched O'Haver the following day.[52] Shelby County jail reports make no mention of Missouri being processed. Surely, Memphis officials informed Missouri of the charge against her, but because she had a small child, they may have allowed her to remain under house arrest.

When these events of early May transpired, Missouri and Isaac had not seen each other for three months. All they had left were their memories of the past Christmas season and their hopes for a summer's reunion. They had dared to defy society's rules, and now an angry society demanded a harsh retribution, one that would take away even more of their freedom and force them to endure the bitter chill of an even longer separation.

5

COLOR LINE JUSTICE

The indictment of Missouri and Isaac for unlawful cohabitation reflected Tennessee's long history of opposition to formal interracial relationships. As early as 1741, while operating largely under the laws of North Carolina, the governing body of the sector that would become Tennessee adopted North Carolina's antimiscegenation provision. The measure explicitly forbade whites from intermarrying with "Indians, Negroes, Mustees [presumably persons of mixed Indian–white heritage] and Mulattoes," and defined persons of "mixed blood" as individuals with one-eighth Indian or African heritage. The statute imposed a fine of fifty pounds for violators and subjected the same penalty on the minister or justice of the peace who performed the nuptials.[1]

During the 1820s, in response to the questions surrounding the expansion of slavery into the Louisiana Territory and the growing number of free blacks throughout the nation, several states enacted new measures to prohibit marriage between blacks and whites. Tennessee was among them. In 1822 the state legislature established its own comprehensive antimiscegenation law. The new measure maintained the same list of groups denied the right to marry whites as the previous statute had done—

with the exception of Indians ("mustees" were still among the restricted groups). In addition, the law retained punishments for government officials, including clerks and/or deputy clerks of the county court who "knowingly" assisted interracial couples in formalizing their unions. Unlike the earlier edict, however, the 1822 law outlawed cohabitation. The penalty for any party abetting an interracial relationship was five hundred dollars, an amount that could be recovered by anyone who entered a suit against them.[2]

Although the 1822 law did not prevent interracial sex in the state, it did effectively frustrate interracial couples who attempted to have public, domestic relationships. Such couples had to stay below the public radar. This was a task most easily accomplished in white male–black female associations, for society gave white men the power to own slave women and to use them sexually with relative impunity. If white men did risk punishments for interracial romances, it usually happened when they tried to sustain them as long-term, meaningful relationships rather than as insignificant sexual flings.[3] For example, in the 1837 case of *Richmond v. Richmond,* a white woman successfully sued her husband for divorce by charging that he had committed adultery with Polly, his slave. Richmond vehemently denied the charges and appealed his case to the Supreme Court of Tennessee, claiming that the divorce had been granted on purely circumstantial evidence. However, the court held that while the evidence was indeed circumstantial, it was still strong enough to affirm the earlier ruling. The high court laid out the following scenario as support for its adjudication:

In this state of things he [Richmond] established his shop in Nashville, several miles from his residence in the county. He took up his residence in his shop in town and took the girl, Polly, with whom the adultery is charged, to keep house for him. He visited his family but seldom, scarcely once a week. He was in the habit of sitting by the fire with Polly after the laborers in the shop had gone to bed.... When these facts are considered in connection with the fact that Hamilton saw him sitting on her bed in the country and hugging her, that Mrs. Bins saw him undressed in the act of rising from the pallet on which Polly slept, and that Alley saw them near each other in the house in town, he buttoning up his pantaloons, and she brushing down her disordered and rumpled dress, it must be admitted that the jury were warranted in finding that they had committed adultery.[4]

Although Richmond's interracial affair led to the public shame of a divorce, there is no record of him being prosecuted under the state's antimiscegenation law. His white, male privilege probably shielded him from such prosecution. However, when black men and white women dared to breach the color line, the state moved quickly to reimpose its notion of order, as it did in the case in *State v. Brady*. In 1848 the state convicted Jesse Brady, a mulatto man, and Louisa Scott, a white woman, of unlawful cohabitation. The judge ordered Scott to pay the five-hundred-dollar fine but waived the penalty for Brady. In the judge's opinion, the 1822 law allowed punishments only for a white man or white woman involved in interracial coupling. Dissatisfied with the judge's interpretation of the law, the state's attorney general appealed to the Tennessee Supreme Court, which, after reviewing the case, affirmed the lower-court ruling. The state high court described the antimiscegenation law as "highly penal" and subject to a strict construction. It concluded that "the loose and careless phraseology" of the law referring to "each and every of the parties" in an interracial relationship being subject to a five-hundred-dollar fine could not practically have applied to slaves. Therefore, it was the "intention" of the state legislature to treat the white man or white woman alone as the "offending party."[5]

The legal conclusions in *State v. Brady* meant that in practice the Tennessee antimiscegenation law existed to punish white women for sustaining interracial relationships.[6] Because in most cases during the antebellum period, African Americans were the slaves of white men, the state relieved blacks of the burden of being fined in order to protect the economic interests of white men. This did not mean, however, that blacks ran no risk in attempting to couple across the color line. To the contrary, that the law did not subject blacks to legal penalties suggests that blacks had very few if any legal protections from the extralegal attempts to control their behavior. The case of *Bloomer v. State* (1855) illustrates this reality all too clearly. On November 1, 1852, James Bloomer, assaulted John Minor by threatening to cut his throat with a knife held within striking distance. Bloomer confessed to the assault but suggested that his actions were justified because Minor was a man of color who sought to marry Bloomer's white, underage, female relative.

The judge in the case did not allow Bloomer to present the marital evidence (including a marriage license Minor had obtained) or to prove that Minor fell within the state's definition of a colored person. However, the judge must have suspected that Minor had African heritage because after the jury found Bloomer guilty, the judge merely fined him one cent plus court costs.[7]

The sectional crisis of the 1850s caused Tennessee leaders to further tighten controls on free blacks. Fearful that free blacks might become pawns of northern abolitionists and encourage slave insurrections, southern authorities passed a number of measures designed to circumscribe the rights of the free black community. Tennessee legislators, along with those in four other southern states, even went so far as to allow free blacks to choose voluntary enslavement. Enacted on March 3, 1858, the Tennessee voluntary enslavement statute empowered any free black eighteen years of age or older to choose a master and petition to become a slave. Once a court had examined each party mentioned in the petition separately to ensure that no fraud was involved, the petitioner and all of his property would then fall into the possession of the designated master. The petitioner and any children born to him after the granting of his request would "in all respects be the same as though such negro had been born a slave."[8]

In 1857–58 the Tennessee legislature also revised the state's antimiscegenation law as part of its attempt to further disenfranchise free blacks. Although very similar to the 1822 provision, the amended statute dropped "mustees" from the groups prohibited from intermarrying with whites and made it impossible for children of interracial couples to inherit their father's property unless the father was a person of color.[9] The inheritance proscription probably came in large part as a reaction to court decisions such as *Ford v. Ford* (1846), which stipulated that a white man could execute a will in favor of his illegitimate biracial children, conferring upon them both emancipation and real estate.[10]

After the Civil War, Tennessee underwent Republican Reconstruction a bit sooner than did other southern states. Instead of directly defying Republican policies, Tennessee leaders grudgingly accepted them, going so far as to ratify the Fourteenth Amendment as early as July 1866. In adopting this strategy of cooperation, Tennessee authorities hoped to ward off stiffer future measures by Radicals in Congress. Their actions proved prescient, for when the Radicals implemented a more stringent Reconstruction plan for the former Confederate states, Tennessee was exempted from its provisions.[11]

Tennessee's temperate manipulation of Republican policies during the 1860s did not translate into full civil equality for African Americans. In fact, in the year that the state ratified the Fourteenth Amendment, blacks could not vote, serve on juries, or attend white schools. Although Tennessee leaders would remove the restrictions on voting and jury service by 1868, blacks still had very limited political power at the state and county levels.[12]

At no time during Reconstruction did the Republican-controlled state legislature or courts remove or invalidate Tennessee's antimiscegenation law. In fact, it appears that throughout that brief era, state authorities maintained their vigilance against interracial coupling. Also, because of their recent emancipation and enfranchisement, African Americans became culpable for violations. On July 19, 1866, the *Nation,* a nationally circulated magazine, reported that a white male–black female couple living in Nashville were fined five hundred dollars for violating the antimiscegenation law, along with the black pastor who performed their wedding. A month later the *Nashville Republican Banner* carried the story of John and Mary Hendricks, an alleged interracial couple who had been apprehended and brought before a local judge. After his careful inspection of Mary, the judge concluded that she was indeed a white person and set the couple free.[13]

The Democratic Party won back control of the state legislature in the 1869 statewide elections. A year later the state constructed a new constitution. At that time public sentiment against interracial marriage and cohabitation was so strong that Tennessee did what few other states would ever do: it placed an antimiscegenation provision in the constitution. Article 11 of section 14 stipulated: "The intermarriage of white persons with negroes, mulattoes, or persons of mixed blood, descended from a negro to the third generation, inclusive, or their living together as man and wife in this state is prohibited. The Legislature shall enforce this section by appropriate legislation."[14]

Shortly after putting the antimiscegenation measure in the constitution, the legislature passed a revised law. The new statute maintained the same groups prohibited from intermarrying with whites found in the 1857–58 laws yet elevated the offense from a misdemeanor to a felony that carried the penalty of imprisonment in the penitentiary for "not less than one nor more than five years." The new law also allowed judges and juries further latitude in meting out punishments. The court could substitute an unspecified fine and term of imprisonment in the county jail for convicted persons in lieu of time in the penitentiary.[15]

With a new, more punitive antimiscegenation law on the books, Tennessee authorities wasted little time in implementing it. In 1871 the state convicted James and Mollie Robertson, a black male–white female couple, for marrying across the color line. The couple appealed their case, citing an improperly worded indictment, but the Supreme Court of Tennessee upheld the decision.[16]

In that same year the Tennessee high court issued a much lengthier decision in a case involving Doc Lonas, a man of color, and Rebecca Teaster, his white lover. The couple had been convicted at the lower-court level and sentenced to two and a half years in the state penitentiary. Lonas appealed his conviction on the grounds that the Thirteenth and Fourteenth Amendments and the Civil Rights Act of 1866 had invalidated the state's antimiscegenation law. As in most other southern states where the question of the constitutionality of antimiscegenation edicts arose, the Tennessee Supreme Court vehemently disagreed. The justices argued that marriage was not an ordinary contract, nor was the right of intermarriage "a privilege or immunity of citizens of the United States as provided for in the Fourteenth Amendment." In this view, the institution of marriage existed under the auspices of the police powers of the states. Thus, the states alone had the right to regulate marriage in accordance with the demands of "domestic peace" and the "public welfare."[17]

The Tennessee Supreme Court further undergirded its decision by employing Bible passages and contending that antimiscegenation laws operated in the best interest of the nation. The court quoted Genesis 24:3, in which Abraham said, "Thou shalt not take a wife into my son of the daughters of the Canaanites among whom I dwell," as a biblical support of the antimiscegenation statute. The high court also declared: "The laws of civilization demand that the races be kept apart in the country. The progress of either does not depend upon an admixture of blood. A sound philanthropy, looking to the public peace and the happiness of both races, would regard any effort to intermerge the individuality of the races as a calamity fall of the saddest and gloomiest potent to the generations that are come after us."[18]

So hostile was the Tennessee judicial system to interracial unions that it did not even matter whether the couple had been residents of another state, married legally while there, and had then migrated to Tennessee. Such couples were still arrested and prosecuted. In 1872 the state's high court reviewed the case of a white man and black woman who had legally married in Mississippi sometime after 1869 and then moved to the state. The couple argued that the legality of their marriage in the state where it was solemnized shielded them from conviction under Tennessee's antimiscegenation statute. However, the Tennessee Supreme Court disagreed, holding that each state retained sovereignty over marriage and had the power to "maintain its own political economy for the good of its citizens." Therefore, Tennessee could forbid "revolting" and "unnatural" interracial coupling within its borders regardless of its acceptance in other states.[19]

By the time that Missouri and Isaac married in late December 1883, the state of Tennessee had established a consistent opposition to interracial relationships. Also, as mentioned in the previous chapter, just prior to Missouri and Isaac's indictment, a Shelby County grand jury had brought charges against James Chambers and Nannie Bennett, another interracial couple. The state placed both Chambers and Bennett on trial in late February 1884. Instead of attempting a crafty defense, Chambers and Bennett pleaded guilty to the charge of unlawful cohabitation and threw themselves on the mercy of the court. After finding the couple guilty, the jury assessed them the quite lenient sentences of three months each in the country jail and court costs. The jury ordered Chambers' incarceration to begin immediately but suspended Bennett's judgment because of the couple's infant child.[20] The Shelby County jail reports reveal that Chambers did spend three months in jail but was not officially released. Instead, he escaped from a chain gang on May 21, 1884.[21]

While awaiting the arrival of Memphis police captain George O'Haver for extradition, Isaac, too, escaped from jail.[22] As he absconded by way of Greenville, Mississippi, Desha County officials alerted authorities throughout the tristate area. In less than a week after his jail break, law enforcement officers in Greenville apprehended him and notified O'Haver. By May 15, 1884, O'Haver had retrieved Isaac and placed him in the Shelby County jail.[23]

Missouri and Isaac would be tried separately. Isaac's day in court came first. It was set for Friday, May 23, 1884. His case was one of seven to be heard that same day before

Judge James M. Greer.[24] Judge Greer had no distinguished political or legal career. He was not listed among the notables in the Shelby County Biographical Index found in *Goodspeed's History of Tennessee* (1887). The forty-year-old attorney and father of four was a one-term criminal court judge of Shelby County, whose time in office was set to expire in August 1884.[25] Interestingly, as mentioned earlier, Greer would go on to successfully represent Ida B. Wells in her suit against the Chesapeake and Ohio and Southwestern Railroad Company in September of that same year.

Shelby County District Attorney General G. P. M. Turner was another important figure in the trial. Turner had been born in Tennessee but moved early in his life to Texas. After reaching adulthood, Turner lived with his family in Mississippi, where he first engaged in the newspaper publishing business. Turner published a paper known as the *Chronicle* in Kosciusko, Mississippi, and later started a paper called *Turner's Southern Star* at Camden, Arkansas. When the Civil War began, Turner enlisted in the Confederate army and rose to the rank of general, commanding a company of Texas Riflemen. After the war, Turner settled in Memphis, where he founded the *Scimitar,* a daily newspaper, and took up the practice of law. In 1878 Turner ran successfully for the office of attorney general, a position that he retained until 1886.[26]

As he had done before the grand jury that indicted Missouri and Isaac, Arkansas City attorney James D. Coates would serve as the special prosecutor at Isaac's trial. Turner accepted Coates's offer to take up the case because Coates had special knowledge of the defendants as well as a passion for the case that suggested he would work hard for a conviction. Also, the fact that Turner had legal troubles of his own no doubt left him only to happy to turn over some of his responsibilities to Coates. Earlier that year, Turner was accused by Frankie Martin, a Shelby County inmate, of assault and battery. Subsequently, the state brought charges against him, tried him in Judge Greer's court, and found him guilty. Greer sentenced Turner to a fine and imprisonment in the county jail. On May 12, the Tennessee Supreme Court reviewed Turner's case on appeal and upheld the verdict and sentence. Fortunately for Turner, he would be pardoned by Governor William B. Bate on May 28, 1884.[27]

If Turner's personal legal problems, among other reasons, made him inclined to allow Coates to handle the case, Coates's own motives are more of a mystery. One can only speculate about why he took such an active interest in prosecuting Isaac. Although it is possible that the Arkansas City attorney was simply a crusader with a strong moral opposition to interracial marriage, it seems more likely that his special interest in the case derived from some personal enmity toward Isaac and/or a desire to advance his own lackluster career. Maybe the two men had been rivals for Missouri's affections. Perhaps Coates envied the success and popularity that Isaac had achieved in Desha County politics. By playing a conspicuous role in a case that was sure to garner ample press coverage, Coates may have hoped to extinguish Isaac's stardom while boosting his own public reputation.

As for Isaac, prior to his arraignment on May 17, 1884, he had a choice of how he could deal with the charge of unlawful cohabitation. He could follow the lead of Chambers and Bennett, plead guilty, and hope for a lenient penalty. Yet, such a strategy was risky. Juries had the legislated authority to sentence a person found guilty of the cohabitation offense to five years in the state penitentiary. Or, Isaac could plead not guilty and attack the antimiscegenation law at its most vulnerable point: the state had to prove beyond a reasonable doubt that the accused individuals fell within the definition of those groups prohibited from marrying.

Isaac chose to plead not guilty. His decision to challenge his own racial classification may have derived from some knowledge of how other interracial couples had successfully avoided convictions by confounding the courts with their diverse racial compositions. For example, in Texas in 1880 a Jefferson County jury convicted Mary Moore of unlawful marriage, only to have the Texas Court of Criminal Appeals reverse the decision in part because of the state's failure to establish Moore's race. The appeals court refused to endorse a two-year prison sentence for Moore on the basis of a single witness's opinion that she looked like a white woman.[28] In the Virginia case of *McPherson v. Commonwealth* (1877), the state supreme court overturned the conviction of George Stewart and Rowena McPherson on the grounds that McPherson had less African heritage than was necessary to be classified as black. According to the court, if McPherson had "but one drop less [of Negro blood], she is not a Negro."[29] In 1883, in another Virginia case, Martha Gray and Isaac Jones, whose marriage license listed them as "black," were indicted for unlawful marriage, with the state claiming that Gray was a white woman. In his defense, Jones argued that his mixed racial heritage made him something other than a "Negro." Gray and Jones lost their case at the lower-court level, but the Virginia high court reversed the decision. In the opinion of the majority of the justices, "it is necessary to establish first, that the accused is a person with one fourth or more Negro blood, that is, that he is a negro; unless this is proved the offence is not proved."[30] By exposing their multiple heritages, interracial couples not only circumvented antimiscegenation laws but also revealed the arbitrary nature of state efforts to impose racial classifications.

Was Isaac in fact racially diverse, or was his claim at trial to be such simply a pragmatic attempt to escape conviction? The answer is unclear. Records indicate that he lived and was treated as a white man for most of his life. Every census lists him as white. He fought for the Confederacy in an all-white Mississippi unit. He ran for and won public office as a white man, and he married a white woman. Yet, some indicators raise the possibility that he could have been racially complex. He aligned with the political party that African Americans associated with during and after Reconstruction. He had important and apparently close ties with prominent African Americans in his community. He established an intimate relationship with a woman of color whom he eventually married. Also, two eyewitnesses commented upon meeting him for the first time that they believed him to be a man of color. Living in a society where one's perceived racial make-up largely determined the degree of freedom an individual possessed, Isaac's parents or grandparents could have made the decision to pass as whites long before Isaac's birth. Having lighter skin tones would have made such a choice possible.[31]

Isaac could have possessed African or Native American heritage—or both—but when defending himself at trial, he classified himself as a Native American, or "Indian," to use the actual language of the era. Why? Perhaps this claim merely reflected what Isaac knew to be his heritage. However, it is possible that he made a practical choice based on what he knew about popular perceptions of native peoples, as opposed to African Americans, and the legal implications of publicly aligning oneself with either group. During the eighteenth and nineteenth centuries, southern white attitudes toward Native Americans underwent a number of changes. In the early 1700s, European settlers recognized them as key players in the social and economic life of what was then the Colonial South. Despite some mutual suspicions, each group acknowledged the interdependent nature of their relationship. Historians have described the interactions between Native Americans and whites in this period as a "middle ground" in which these varied cultures assimilated with and transformed one another.[32]

As the century progressed and more English settlers migrated to the region, a counter-ideology emerged that challenged the "middle ground" idea. According to Joel Martin, southern whites began more and more to view Native Americans as savages. This mind-set stemmed from the declining dependence of Europeans on trade with Native Americans, the growing desire for native lands, and the defeat of the French in the French and Indian War and their subsequent departure. The growing notion of "native savages" significantly affected how English settlers dealt with Native Americans. Instead of encouraging assimilation, white colonials now preferred to marginalize and displace native peoples—a tendency that would only increase as the decades passed.[33]

Although the English had been more cooperative with Native Americans at the beginning of the eighteenth century than they would be toward the end of it, the English, unlike the French, had never viewed indigenous persons as acceptable marriage partners. Most of the early antimiscegenation laws listed Indians among the prohibited groups. However, the English reluctance to intermarry with Native Americans derived less from any notion of their biological inferiority than from a perception of their cultural backwardness. In the English mind, Native Americans were heathens who lacked proper manners, dress, and other attributes befitting so-called civilized society.[34] Also, the early English colonials proscribed marriage between whites and Native Americans as a way of limiting the sexual choices of white women. Because of the significant demographic shortages of white women, especially at the beginning of the century, colonial legislators sought to ensure that Englishmen would have full access to English women in order to produce English families.[35]

During the early nineteenth century, southern whites continued to see Native Americans as savages—but with some ambivalence. To those southerners on the coastal plains where the indigenous tribes had been removed, Native Americans possessed a certain measure of nobility. They were seen as inherently good people who suffered because of their cultural backwardness. They simply needed more contact with whites in order to learn and assume the "proper" ways of living. For those southern whites who had settled farther inland, however, Native Americans were savages pure and simple. Coveting native lands, these white southerners believed that pushing Native Americans farther west—which Congress and President Andrew Jackson would ultimately do through the Indian Removal Act—was the proper way of dealing with them.[36]

By the time that Missouri and Isaac married, Native Americans were no longer a threat in the South. As a result, late-nineteenth-century white southerners tended to see them as representative of some dreamy, mythical, romantic past. This helps to explain in part why Native Americans lost their place among the prohibited groups in many southern antimiscegenation laws. Now that southern whites had displaced and largely exterminated native tribes, they could afford to view them in some "deep sense" as ancestors. Southern rivers, towns, and mountains could carry native names, and possessing some native blood was no liability for a white southerner.[37]

African Americans conceptualized Native Americans in ways that helped them psychologically confront segregation and discrimination. For blacks, Native Americans represented resistance to the so-called civilizing influences of white society. To those African Americans who could claim native ancestors, this meant that they believed they were capable of and naturally inclined toward defying the racial caste system imposed by Jim Crow laws and customs. Furthermore, having Native American heritage in practice gave blacks greater potential access to the services and opportunities that whites enjoyed. In the 1880s many institutions and businesses that refused to cater to blacks accepted Native Americans. Booker T. Washington, the famous black leader and head of the Tuskegee Institute in Alabama, recalled in *Up From Slavery* an incident that illustrated the greater rights that Native Americans had in America's caste system. While teaching at Virginia's Hampton Normal and Agricultural Institute in 1880, Washington was required to escort one of his Native American charges to Washington,

D.C. On two separate occasions, in a steamboat dining room and at a Washington hotel, the educator was informed that the Native American could be served while he would be required to find other accommodations.[38] By accentuating Native American heritage, blacks with the requisite appearance could sometimes circumvent Jim Crow laws and more effectively negotiate the color line.

Isaac recognized that in defending himself against the charge of unlawful marriage, prudence required him to claim Native American heritage. He could not deny the fact of the marriage to Missouri because of the evidence of the license. However, he could complicate the state's effort to establish his racial identity as white. Even if Isaac had African ancestry, sound reasoning suggested that he deny it. Although claiming blackness would have exonerated him from the charge of unlawful cohabitation with Missouri, he would have risked making himself culpable for a similar charge in Arkansas because of his marriage to Martha. Also, Isaac's children with Martha would then have had to suffer economically and socially. If Isaac had been deemed a person of African descent, his children, Isaac Jr. and Laura, would have been legally bastardized because of their parent's unlawful relationship and severely compromised in their right to inherit his property. Furthermore, as long as they remained in or near Desha County, the children would have had to bear the heavy burden of being designated "descendants of Africans."

Isaac's trial took place on May 31, 1884, a warm and clear Saturday. Eleven jurors were chosen to hear the seven cases set for that day. All of the jurors were men with no fewer than four of them having white-collar occupations: Thomas Graham, Fenton D. Craig, and Samuel B. Williamson worked as clerks, while James C. Bell was a bookkeeper. Although most of the jurors were white, one of them, Henry Hoss, was of African descent. The *Memphis City Directory* listed Hoss as "colored" and his occupation as policeman in 1883.[39]

Coates summoned two witnesses for the state, Abe Manley and Cornelia Winston.[40] Unless he had known Isaac personally, Manley, a blacksmith, would have testified to having seen Missouri and Isaac riding into town together and caring for their horses. Winston would have answered questions about the couple lodging together as husband and wife. The execution docket did not indicate whether the defense called any witnesses.

The *Arkansas Gazette*'s account of the trial noted that Coates went to great lengths in his attempts to prove that Isaac was a white man, but unfortunately, the newspaper offered no details about the attorney's specific arguments or tactics. Frustrated in his efforts, Coates became, as the *Gazette* put it, more "malicious" in his prosecution.[41] District Attorney General Turner eventually rose to his feet to stop the case, declaring that the prosecution "had not made his case" and asked Greer to instruct the jury to find Isaac "not guilty." Turner also urged Judge Greer to charge Coates with court costs.[42] Greer adhered to Turner's requests, and despite the apparent absence of defense witnesses, Isaac escaped conviction.[43]

Why was the court so agreeable to Isaac's defense? Isaac had spent his entire life accepting the social construction of whiteness; yet the court acquitted him for alleging to be Native American. Although Isaac's physical appearance more than likely aided his cause, other factors must have played a role. As mentioned earlier, white males had sexual privileges that other groups did not share. Perhaps the all-male officers of the court felt a certain affinity for Isaac and wanted to embrace any defense that would exonerate him. It must be remembered that in the earlier Shelby County case, *State v. Chambers and Bennett*, Chambers admitted guilt and received a relatively light sentence. White men could be prosecuted for violating antimiscegenation laws, but generally courts applied the statutes more rigidly in cases involving relationships between white women and black men.

Turner may have also had other reasons why he so blatantly imposed his influence in the case. He was an elected official who had been convicted for misconduct. Maybe he felt some compassion for Isaac after having gone through his own ordeal. Perhaps Turner recognized that black Memphians probably frowned upon antimiscegenation laws because of the negative assumptions they made about African heritage. By exonerating Isaac and subsequently Missouri, Turner could better pander to the black electorate. Turner definitely cared about how the black community viewed him because in the year following the trial, he became the first district attorney general in the county's history to appoint an African American as an assistant prosecutor. That man was Josiah J. T. Settle, a lawyer and former student at Howard University.[44]

Finally, Turner's readiness to intervene on Isaac's behalf may have derived from some special affinity he had for Native Americans. Both of Turner's sons, G. H. Turner and Scott Turner, would as adults migrate to and live in Indian

Territory. In fact, the former was eventually elected mayor of Checotah Oaks, Indian Territory. And at the time of his death in 1900, G. P. M. Turner himself was also residing in Indian Territory. His family buried him in what is now Muskogee, Oklahoma.[45]

From a legal perspective, a question about the whole episode remains: why was there no effort, in either Arkansas or Tennessee, to charge Missouri and Isaac with bigamy? After all, Isaac was still married to Martha Bankston when he and Missouri ran off to Memphis. For Arkansas law enforcement, the answer to the question is clear. The state's high court had ruled that an indictment for bigamy could only be brought in the county where the offense had occurred. Because Missouri and Isaac had married in Shelby County, Tennessee, they were outside the jurisdiction of Arkansas law.[46]

With regard to Tennessee, the reasons behind no charges of bigamy are less clear. The wording of the state's legal code seemed sufficient to make Isaac, at least, culpable for such a violation. It was an offense in Tennessee for a married person to wed someone else when the original spouse was alive in the United States and had been accessible within a five-year period. Yet, Tennessee made no obvious attempt to prosecute Isaac for bigamy. Why? The answer may be tied to the fact that Tennessee law required authorities to enter the license from the first marriage as evidence against the accused. Isaac had married Martha in Mississippi prior to the Civil War. Tennessee authorities were probably not privy to that information, and it is doubtful that Isaac would have told them about it. As for Missouri, Tennessee officials would have found it difficult to convict her of bigamy because the state code required proof that she had wed Isaac with full knowledge of his existing marital status—something that Missouri could easily deny.[47]

There was scant coverage of the court's verdict on the day after the trial. Nothing about it appeared in the *Memphis Daily Appeal,* while the *Arkansas Gazette* presented only a brief, matter-of-fact summary of what had transpired. Isaac had escaped conviction, but this outcome carried a steep price. Isaac was forced to admit in public that he had long deceived family, friends, and supporters on two fronts—first, about his relationship with a colored woman and, second, about his connection to the white race. Now the people in Isaac's world knew by his own confession that he belonged on the colored side of the color line. Isaac undoubtedly recognized that his life would never be the same—a thought that must have deeply disturbed him. Although Isaac had chosen to marry Missouri, somehow he felt that the problems he encountered, the shame that had come to Martha and his children as a result of his actions, were the fault of others. Principally, he blamed James Coates, and he intended to extract some measure of revenge from him.

6

A QUEST FOR HONOR

On the day following Isaac's trial, the *Memphis Daily Appeal* reported on an incident in Batesville, Mississippi, involving two white men, H. W. Thaten, editor of the *Batesville Blade,* and a young lawyer named Julius Porter. According to the article, Thaten had insinuated that Porter was responsible for a number of thefts in local businesses. Outraged by the accusation, Porter demanded that Thaten publish a retraction. Thaten refused. On the morning of May 31, 1884, Porter approached Thaten on the streets of the city with a drawn pistol as Thaten made his way to his office at the *Blade.* Porter yelled for Thaten to defend himself and immediately fired two or three shots. None of them hit Thaten, who drew his own weapon and fired at Porter, hitting him just above the thigh. Porter clasped his wound, turned to retreat, and fired two more shots at Thaten, again missing his target. As Porter attempted to run away, Thaten followed him, nearly emptying his gun. When Porter fell, Thaten stood over him prepared to fire his last shot, but bystanders stopped him. Soon afterward, Porter died on the street from his wounds.[1]

The fatal confrontation between Thaten and Porter was fairly typical of the post-Reconstruction South. Vestiges of the pre–Civil War period in which formal dueling and street brawling were accepted parts of the social structure, these violent encounters revealed the belief of many southerners that an individual had not only the right but an obligation to avenge personal, public slanders against his character and name. Historians have disagreed about the roots of southern violence. Some have emphasized the frontier character of the region, suggesting that the rugged individualism cultivated by life in the backwoods encouraged the use of force in resolving conflicts.[2] Others have argued that individual violence in the South stemmed from the region's economic reliance on slavery and its hypersensitivity to the possibility of insurrection and race war.[3] Still others have offered that southerners so readily resorted to violence because of their fears of excessive individual passions that contravened long-held traditions or norms. According to this theory, southerners viewed inordinate individual passions as a serious threat to the social order and the use of violence as a means to keep them in check.[4] For example, if excessive lust led a man to impregnate a woman who was not his wife, society required him to marry the woman. If he did not, southern society permitted violence against the man to discourage others from following a similar course.

Regardless of the theory as to the roots of violence, historians agree that the issue of honor played a central role in triggering southerners to employ it. According to Bertram Wyatt-Brown, honor "was an encoded system, a matter of interchanges between the individual and the community to which he or she belonged. Meaning was imparted not with words alone, but in courtesies, rituals and even deeds of personal and collective violence." In other words, southerners embraced a set of cultural rules that they believed all people should follow. As long as the individual abided by those societal values, he or she could live honorably. However, when an individual rejected community norms, it created the strong likelihood that he would invite shame himself and/or others. This public sentiment could not be ignored. It was important for all persons affected by the humiliation to ensure that it was corrected. The failure to do so could mean forfeited honor to all involved.[5]

Southerners so esteemed the notion of honor that many considered its loss more disastrous than death. Within such a mind-set, unrequited public humiliation was totally unacceptable. Not only was an unresolved public affront viewed as a cancer that threatened the family body, but it was also seen as a congenital defect that crippled unborn posterity. Family members had an absolute moral obligation to maintain and protect their honor and thus preserve the clan's social reputation.[6]

The South's conception of honor often required gender-specific behavior. Southern women were supposed to manifest such traits as restraint, contentment, chastity, and submissiveness, while southern men were to demonstrate assertiveness, dominance, aggressiveness, and valor. In practice, this suggested that men were to lead forcefully, and women were to follow. A "proper" husband might accept the advice of his wife, but a "proper" wife would always suppress any desire to question her husband's authority.[7]

With regard to sex, the southern honor code also mandated gendered behavior. Sexual virtue mattered much more for women than for men. Southern men could and often did have lovers prior to marriage. They often entered into sexual liaisons with women other than their wives.

Such broaches of religious and rhetorical calls to chastity and fidelity did not necessarily destroy a man's reputation. In fact, southern society almost expected it. However, women were given no sexual leeway. From them, society required strict adherence to ideas of sexual purity. If a woman had sexual encounters with a man, or several men, prior to marriage, she was considered damaged goods—something lewd and akin to a harlot. Such pejorative labeling not only reduced her options for marriage, but they negatively affected her family's reputation as well.[8]

Although the southern honor code had always demanded that male family members secure the sexual integrity of women, whites in the postwar South began to perceive the need for such protection through racial lenses. Increasingly, black men became the focus of whites in their sometimes violent efforts to preserve the honor of wives, mothers, and sisters. The heightened tendency of whites to view black men as threats derived largely from the emancipation of blacks and white fears of social leveling. Despite maintaining their own access to black women, white men insisted that black men leave white women alone. Black men who crossed the sexual color line in any way could trigger the violent responses of white men.[9]

The lynching of African Americans, especially men, became a social phenomenon after the Civil War. Though lynch mobs could form for any transgression, their most common justification was to protect white female virtue. Whites claimed that they lynched black men to punish those who raped white women and to discourage others who might do so.[10]

Lynching could be an elaborate public spectacle that attracted thousands of onlookers or a more private affair that involved a handful of people from a small community. During the time that Missouri and Isaac had their relationship, lynching was becoming more commonplace in Arkansas and throughout the South. In July 1881 the *Arkansas Gazette* reported on one such incident in the town of Georgia, Arkansas. According to the news article, a black man named Peter Henderson allegedly entered the home of a Mr. and Mrs. Harris, a white couple, while Mr. Harris was away. Henderson was said to have slipped into Mrs. Harris's bed without her knowledge. When she awoke, the woman screamed for help, at which point Henderson choked her (though not to death) and then fled the house. Local whites later captured Henderson, who confessed. Despite the claim of local blacks that Henderson was "touched in the head," his captors apparently killed him. It was certain, the paper commented, that Henderson would never again disturb the "virtual couch" of any white woman "by his midnight intrusions."[11]

One year later in July 1882, the *Arkansas Gazette* recounted the story of Eli Mckiney, a twenty-three-year-old mulatto, who reportedly attempted to rape a white woman in Arkadelphia, Arkansas. According to the paper, the woman's screams alerted her faithful dog, which successfully rescued her from "this brute of a negro." Later that evening, an "unknown party" captured Mckiney and castrated him. The paper asserted that such actions were justified to protect the "innocence" of daughters and mothers.[12]

Black men did not have to be accused of raping white women to experience violent reprisals. Sometimes white men attacked black men involved in consensual relationships with white women. In December 1879 a Texas paper, the *Marshal Tri-Weekly Herald,* told of Mary and Henry

Moore, an interracial couple who had lived together for several years before authorities apprehended them. During the arrest, Mary was taken peacefully, but a deputy sheriff "was forced to shoot" Henry, "perhaps fatally," for attempting to run away.[13] In Pine Bluff, Arkansas, in March 1881, authorities took Thomas Kilpatrick, a white man, into custody for allegedly firing a shotgun at Frank Young, a black man who lived with a white woman, as Young sat in the door of his home. Kilpatrick vehemently denied the charge, and the newspaper account mentioned that he would soon be released.[14] Also, in a similar case in Pulaski County, Arkansas, a black resident name Jerry Meyers accused two white men, John Darnell and Homer Owens, of dragging him from his home, tying him to a tree, and severely whipping him. According to Meyers, his marriage to a white woman had prompted the beating. Authorities arrested Darnell and Owens, questioned them, and then let them go after they denied the accusation.[15]

Even if a black man insinuated that a white woman had a bad character, the remark could cost him his life. Such was the case of a black man named Hill who lived near Memphis in 1884. Hill supposedly accused the wife of C. A. Bartliffe, a white plantation owner for whom Hill worked, of having an affair with a white man on a nearby farm. Bartliffe was away on business when Hill first made the charge, but upon his return, Bartliffe sought out Hill, found him walking on a public road, and without hesitation or concern for witnesses, shot him four times, killing him. Bartliffe was arrested, but the *Memphis Daily Appeal* reported that public opinion among both blacks and whites supported his actions. In fact, even Hill's stepmother supposedly said that "she did not blame Mr. Bartliffe for protecting his wife's good name."[16]

The paper may have exaggerated the degree to which blacks favored Bartliffe's attack on Hill, but it did not misrepresent the southern black community's embrace of notions of honor. Even during antebellum times, slaves had their own honor codes that recognized male chivalry and encouraged monogamous relationships. However, premarital sex that produced children did not carry the same social stigma among slaves that it did for southern whites. After the Civil War, African Americans increasingly advocated middle-class values of temperance and chastity for women. For blacks as well as whites, an honorable woman kept her sexual virtue and a noble man protected it.[17] Whites, however, viewed blacks as inherently immoral. In the minds of whites, the innate character of black men and women made it virtually impossible for them to live honorably without strict external controls. Black men were thought to be naturally subservient, cowardly, and profligate, while black women were wanton, aggressive, flashy, and crude. To whites, both black men and women were hypersexual "beasts." Therefore, white men felt justified in both their carnal exploitation of black women and their legal and extralegal sexual control of black men. For many whites, African Americans had no honor that they were bound to respect.[18]

Although black men sometimes protected the sexual honor of black women against the untoward advances of white men, they more often punished men of their own race for honor-code breaches against black women and children. In most cases, even after the Civil War, whites rarely punished black men for affronting black women. However, black men who ran afoul of community honor sometimes encountered violence at the hands of other blacks.[19] For example, in December 1882 no less than one hundred armed black men in Varner, Arkansas, overpowered the local sheriff and his deputies to seize Charles B. Branch, a black constable who was accused of sexually assaulting and murdering a nine-year-old black girl. Convinced of Branch's guilt, the men hanged him from a telegraph pole.[20] Black men responded in a similar fashion in July 1885 in Pine Bluff, Arkansas. Local authorities had charged David Scruggs, a black man, with incest and arrested him. After Scruggs was released from jail, black men abducted him and carved him "to pieces with knives." Scruggs subsequently died from his wounds.[21]

* * *

When Isaac's trial ended, he returned to Arkansas City. On Monday, June 2, 1884, Isaac reached the town. The sky was clear and the temperature rising. Court was in session, and James Coates was serving as one of the prosecutors in an arson case. Isaac must have known of Coates's whereabouts because he went directly to the courthouse, carrying a sidearm and a heavy cane. At 4:00 PM Isaac stood on the steps of the courthouse, waiting for Coates to come outside. A small crowd had gathered anxiously, anticipating what they assumed would be a bloody confrontation. Witnesses later commented that Isaac had threatened to kill someone.[22]

When Coates stepped outside the courthouse, Isaac greeted him with an assortment of curses. In fact, one article that covered the event described Isaac's words as "the vilest language imaginable"—a clear indication of how Isaac regarded Coates.[23] Instead of speaking to Coates in the courtly, dignified manner that duelists used, Isaac addressed him as if he were not his social equal.[24] Coates told Isaac that he did not want "any trouble" and attempted to walk away. At this point, Isaac struck Coates with the cane. Coates pulled out a knife and lunged at Isaac, stabbing him in the chest. Isaac dropped his cane and retreated, but at the same time he drew his pistol and fired at Coates, striking him in the chest. The lawyer fell to the ground. Apparently thinking that the fight was done, Isaac turned to walk away. Coates, however, had just enough life left to make one last lunge with his knife, piercing Isaac in the back. Both men collapsed on the courthouse steps. The battle for honor was over.[25]

On the following day, various area papers reported on the violent episode, with the *Arkansas Gazette* providing the most extensive coverage that still remains. Coates died on the courthouse steps. His funeral took place on the evening of June 4. Several of "the best people" were in attendance, and the court and many businesses closed "as a tribute of respect to him."[26] In fact, it appears that Coates's brawl with Isaac increased his popularity among area residents, for prior to the fight he had little acclaim in the community. He never won an election for county office, nor was he mentioned among the leaders of the county in an 1883 article published in the *Arkansas City Journal*. He was far from wealthy. Probate records reveal that, upon his death, he had only $225 in personal property and $57 in outstanding debt.[27] There is no evidence that he owned any real estate. When he died at Isaac's hands, however, business and civic leaders embraced him because he had stood for community values.

Isaac did not die immediately but lingered for two days. After his death, the family buried him in a private ceremony on Walnut Lake. In stark contrast to Coates's funeral, Isaac's burial occurred in relative obscurity, without fanfare or recognition. There was no mention of any notables in attendance. Isaac's decision to cross the color line had caused former friends and supporters to forsake him in death, just as they had done when his marriage to Missouri became public.[28]

On June 14, 1884, the Shelby County Criminal Court officially dismissed the case against Missouri.[29] Isaac's exoneration from unlawful cohabitation charges had also worked to clear her name in the eyes of the law. Now, Missouri would be free to go on with her life. But what life? Isaac was dead, a fact that she doubtless learned from the local papers. This meant that her husband, lover, economic provider, and the father of her child was gone. Missouri would have to make significant emotional, psychological, and practical adjustments. The new demands of her life denied her the luxury of mourning too long. Isaac had left her nothing from his estate. Nor was Missouri legally entitled to any of his possessions. She would once again have to take full responsibility for her own survival and that of her child. At this point, Missouri and her son became lost to historical records.

Martha's Desha County neighbors apparently did not blame the family for Isaac's public shortcomings because Martha never left Walnut Lake. After Isaac's death, she stayed with her children on the farm, serving as the administrator of Isaac's estate.[30] Also, Isaac Jr. served as a deputy from time to time under future county sheriffs.[31] The 1900 federal census reveals that Martha, then fifty-eight years old, continued living on the family land but no longer as head of household. Isaac Jr. had claimed that position, and he lived there with his wife, Mildred, and their two-year-old daughter, Bertie. The exact date of Martha's death is unknown, but the 1900 census is the last one in which she is mentioned.[32]

As adults, Isaac Jr. and Laura also stayed in Desha County. Isaac Jr. married Mildred Metcalf in 1897, and Laura wed Sam R. Stovall in 1896. By 1920 Isaac Jr. and Mildred were living at Walnut Lake with their fifteen-year-old daughter, Mary. Bertie, apparently, had not survived. In that same year, Laura lived as the head of household in the Randolph Township with her four children, Von, Palmer, Sidney, and Martha Elizabeth.[33]

By 1930 much had changed in the life of Isaac Jr. He and Mildred had divorced. Mildred operated a boarding house in Harris County, Texas, where she resided with her daughter, Mary. Apparently, at some point during the 1920s, Mary had married because her last name was listed as Rogers, and she had a six-year-old child named Stella. Meanwhile, Isaac Jr. had remarried. Fifty-seven years old in 1930, he had remained in Walnut Lake, living there with his twenty-two-year-old wife, Ima.[34]

CONCLUSION

Missouri and Isaac's story tells us much about southern norms regarding race and gender in the post-Reconstruction period. By critically analyzing the key characters in this saga, one gains a rich understanding of how race and gender worked within the region's social, economic, and legal milieu. For example, from Isaac's story we learn that southern white men not only had the power to enforce the law but also the ability to evade it. Southern white males had greater access to wealth and political power than did any other group. They controlled southern legislative bodies, courts, and law enforcement. Such authority enabled them to run afoul of the very edicts they enacted (such as the antimiscegenation laws) with relative impunity. Yes, white men could be punished for having black lovers—but only when they had dared to elevate the social status of black women by establishing some level of a formal relationship with them. Even then, as in Isaac's case, white men could still find ways to evade conviction.[1]

An assessment of Missouri reveals both the agency of black women and the limits that southern society placed on them. Missouri convinced Isaac to make her a formal partner. Her insistence and Isaac's acquiescence suggests that black women often crafted personal relationships in self-empowering ways. Missouri probably sought a formal relationship with Isaac at least in part because she believed that it offered her greater financial security. Also, she wanted her child with Isaac to have legitimacy. However, the very factors that motivated Missouri to push Isaac to marry her reflected the social confines under which Missouri and other women of color lived. Black women had few occupational options during the period, and those jobs that were available to them often failed to provide a living wage. Therefore, economic considerations regularly forced black women to rely on men for survival.[2]

Southern white women, too, had economic limitations that prevented them from having greater autonomy and social power. The lives of Isaac's mother, Rosa, and his white wife, Martha, illustrate this point. Like Missouri, Rosa and Martha needed a formal relationship with men to better ensure their financial well-being. This need compelled them to conform to norms that they might have personally detested. It is quite possible that Martha knew of Isaac's affair before it became public, as it was not uncommon for southern white women to remain silent despite knowing that their men had black lovers. Even after Isaac's arrest and trial, Martha stayed in her marriage. She did not dare leave him. Martha simply could not afford to make such a move.[3]

By examining the reactions of Shelby County officials James Lewis, G. P. M. Turner, and James Greer, as well as that of Minister J. E. Roberts, to the coupling of Missouri and Isaac, we learn that race lacked any clear, universal definition in everyday southern life. Although states had antimiscegenation laws that sought to define race, personal observation more than anything else dictated how people determined it. Each of the men mentioned above saw Missouri and Isaac together and assumed they had no racial difference that would impede their relationship. In fact, Lewis and Roberts actually thought that Missouri and Isaac were racially similar. This is not to say that race had no meaning, for it most certainly did. However, southern society had no reliable means of ensuring that individuals accepted the racial definitions the state gave to them. This meant that southerners with racial characteristics that placed them on the edges of racial difference could and would skirt those boundaries.[4]

Missouri and Isaac's story also reveals much about the complex ways that individuals negotiate societal norms to express a measure of personal autonomy. In several respects, sustaining their intimate connection required Missouri and Isaac to defy convention. Despite the social rules that insisted upon an inconspicuous and informal relationship, Missouri and Isaac dared to formalize and consequently to publicize their affections. Their decision to defy societal dictates forced each of them to forsake significant aspects of their former lives. Missouri felt compelled to leave Arkansas City. Sensing the growing community discomfort with her relationship with Isaac, she moved to Memphis, where she could more fully engage him. By remaining with Isaac, Missouri also compromised her association with the black community. Although blacks generally were more willing to accept interracial relationships than whites, African Americans still tended to frown on such liaisons. For many blacks, those in the community who crossed the sexual color line became symbolic expressions of an unspoken desire to escape their racial affiliations.[5]

Isaac, too, gave up much to formalize his connection with Missouri. He strained his relationships with Martha,

Isaac Jr., and Laura. He forfeited his right to political and social prominence, giving up his position as county sheriff and his generally positive reputation in the county. Isaac's relationship with Missouri even legally cost him his whiteness. To escape a conviction for unlawful marriage, Isaac had to deny the very social construction that had empowered him to have greater access to social, economic, and political opportunity.

Yet, Missouri and Isaac's courageous willingness to confront the opposition to their union and to abandon so much in order to retain it does not mean that societal values and conditions failed to influence their decisions. To the contrary, it was Missouri and Isaac's captivity to certain community ideas and circumstances that ultimately caused them to lose each other. Missouri felt that her relationship with Isaac could ensure her financial security only if they married. Also, like so many other women during her time, she wanted a formal tie to a man to give her child legitimacy. However, by insisting on marriage, Missouri not only made the couple's relationship more public but also gave the state greater legal power to force them apart. For Isaac, the demand that lost honor be avenged proved to be the social standard that determined his actions. After the trial, instead of embracing the new life with Missouri made possible by the verdict, Isaac followed the dictates of the southern honor code and confronted Coates on the steps of the Arkansas City courthouse. Isaac's decision deprived him of his life and his connection to Missouri. When all was said and done, Missouri and Isaac's actions show that although they could forsake others, they could not fully ignore the values that shaped them or the conditions under which each of them lived.

Yet, whatever Isaac and Missouri's own flaws of conformity, it was the larger society that bore the greater blame for this human tragedy. An opprobrious unwillingness to recognize the fundamental equality of African Americans and women lay at the heart of the white South's persistence in embracing norms and adopting laws that mandated racial separation and gender disparity. These laws and customs worked to remind everyone of a southern caste system that put white men at the top and blacks and women below them.

The social attitudes about interracial relationships that determined the experiences of Missouri and Isaac still have a chilling affect on American society. Although today interracial couples can legally wed, many must still often face disapproval. Frequently, interracial couples must witness the stares, grimaces, and other nonverbal indicators of those who are hostile to or uncomfortable with their unions. Similarly, interracial dating and even more casual outings between blacks and whites are viewed with suspicion. As a result, less than 1 percent of all marriages in the United States involve black-white couples.[6] Overall, public attitudes about interracial marriage, though more positive today than at other times in American history, still reflect the sense that people would be better off marrying within their own racial group.

The failure of Americans to make more fundamental changes in their racial perceptions is at the core of this continuing discomfort with black-white relationships. There is no doubting that Americans have adjusted their racial attitudes over the second half of the twentieth century to allow for important institutional changes and to eradicate Jim Crow laws. Today blacks and whites can attend the same schools, use the same public facilities, and engage each other in publicly sociable ways. However, despite establishing the possibility for greater integration, Americans retain much of their segregated past. Neighborhoods, schools, and churches remain largely racially homogenous. When Americans attend integrated functions such as concerts and sporting events, they commonly do so with people from similar racial backgrounds. In state universities and colleges, it is highly unlikely that students will attend classes that mirror the racial demographics of the nation. Even if the institution of higher learning has a relatively strong diversity, students often segregate themselves within classes, fraternities, and sororities. As adults, Americans are for the most part hard pressed to name friends outside of their own racial groups. Perhaps they know one or two people, but rarely do Americans have social circles that suggest a fully open and inclusive society.

The net result of this American proclivity to live within racially defined social circles is a nation that still has trouble with seeing individuals beyond the color of their skin. Americans might frown at the use of racial epithets, condemn conspicuous acts of discrimination, and support programs designed to enhance multiculturalism; but these actions do not mean that Americans have learned to embrace people racially different from themselves and to treat them as social equals. Many Americans still view cultural distinctions as indications of some level of inferiority, especially when such differences are tied to race. Therefore, despite all the rhetoric to the contrary, many Americans remain unwilling to accept the common humanity of all people.

As it was during Missouri and Isaac's time, interracial relationships today suffer because of deliberate acts to discourage and prevent them. In October 2009 a Louisiana interracial couple received national attention when they revealed that a local justice of the peace had refused to marry them. The official justified his refusal by contending that such relationships are difficult on the children they produce and do not last.[7] In less dramatic ways, some parents regularly inform their children, whether directly or subtly, that interracial coupling would not be welcomed. Friends and neighbors add to this dynamic by often delivering negative messages about intimate interracial associations. Even when cohorts declare themselves open to such liaisons, they frequently focus on the special problems that interracial couples experience rather than highlight the benefits that could be gained from such relationships. The overall lesson is that even in modern times, much as in Missouri and Isaac's era, those involved in interracial connections still have to demonstrate the capacity to forsake all others in order to maintain them.

NOTES

Introduction

1. Waldo E. Martin Jr., *The Mind of Frederick Douglass* (Chapel Hill: Univ. of North Carolina Press, 1970), 99; Francis J. Grimke, "Second Marriage of Frederick Douglass," *Journal of Negro History* 19 (July 1934): 324–29; Arna Bontemps, *Free At Last: The Life of Frederick Douglass* (New York: Dodd, Mead & Co., 1971), 276–77; Maria Diedrich, *Love across Color Lines: Ottilie Assing and Frederick Douglass* (New York: Hill and Wang, 1999), 368–69.

2. Bontemps, *Free At Last,* 275–92.

3. U.S. Bureau of the Census, *Tenth Census of the United States, 1880,* Population Schedules, Bolivar County, MS (Washington, DC: National Archives and Records Administration, n.d.), microfilm, T9, roll 641. Unless otherwise noted, subsequent citations of U.S. census records all refer to National Archives microfilms and will give only shortened title references (e.g., *Tenth Census, 1880*), followed by county name, state abbreviation, publication number (e.g., T9, M653), and roll number. All references are to general population schedules unless otherwise stated.

4. *Tenth Census, 1880,* Desha County, AR, T9, roll 43.

1. Mississippi on His Mind

1. Descriptions of morning activities related to the port in Arkansas City can be found in James Merritt, "Arkansas City, A Natural Steamboat Landing," *Programs of Desha County Historical Society* 16 (1991): 13–16.

2. The earliest records of Ignatius Bankston are found on an 1829 Chicot County tax list. See Chicot County Records, Tax Records, 1829–1855, roll 68 (microfilm), Arkansas Historical Commission, Little Rock. See also *Fifth Census, 1830,* Chicot County, Territory of Arkansas, M19, roll 5.

3. Florence Walter Sillers, Regent, and Members of Mississippi Delta Chapter, and Daughters of the American Revolution of Rosedale and Bolivar County, *History of Bolivar County* (Jackson, MS: Hederman Brothers, 1948), 71–77.

4. James C. Cobb, *The Most Southern Place on Earth: The Mississippi Delta and the Roots of Regional Identity* (New York: Oxford Univ. Press, 1992), 7–28.

5. Ibid.

6. For a good description of the area the Bankstons left in the Arkansas Delta, see Williard B. Gatewood, "The Arkansas Delta: The Deepest of the Deep South," in *The Arkansas Delta: Land of Paradox,* ed. Jeannie Whayne and Williard B. Gatewood, 3–29 (Fayetteville: Univ. of Arkansas Press, 1993).

7. Edward Pessen, *Jacksonian America: Society, Personality, and Politics* (Homewood, IL: Dorsey Press, 1969), 154–84; Sillers, *History of Bolivar County,* 5–47, 66. Many of the Bolivar County records for the years 1856–65 have been lost.

8. *Seventh Census, 1850,* Free Schedules, Bolivar County, MS, M432, roll 368; *Eighth Census, 1860,* Free Schedules, Bolivar County, MS, M653, roll 578; General M/F File, Mississippi Counties Tax Records, Bolivar County, 1837–1879, roll 5 (microfilm), Mississippi Dept. of Archives and History, Jackson.

9. *Eighth Census, 1860,* Slave Schedules, Bolivar County, MS, M653, roll 595.

10. General M/F File, Mississippi Counties Tax Records, Bolivar County, 1837–1879, roll 5.

11. Gail Criss and Charlotte Hill, "A Demographic Study of Bolivar County in 1850," and Ann D. Clifton, "A Demographic Study of Bo-

livar County in 1860," *Journal of the Bolivar County Historical Society* 1 (Mar. 1977): 3–9, 10–20. Also see Stephanie McCurry, *Masters of Small Worlds: Yeoman Households, Gender Relations, and the Political Culture of the Antebellum South Carolina Low Country* (New York: Oxford Univ. Press, 1995), 56–61.

12. In 1850 Lafayette Bankston had one slave, an eighteen-year-old male, to assist with the family farm labor. Lafayette would file for a divorce from Angeline in February 1857. Apparently, she had left Lafayette for another man in 1854 and had borne two or three children by him. *Sixth Census, 1840,* Bolivar County, MS, M704, roll 215; *Seventh Census, 1850,* Free Schedules, Bolivar County, MS, M432, roll 368; Katherine Clements Branton and Alice Clements Wade, eds., *Early Mississippi Records: Bolivar County,* vol. 1, *1836–61* (Jackson: Mississippi Dept. of Archives and History, 1988), 158. Also, for additional information about family labor on frontier farms, see Donald P. McNeilly, *The Old South Frontier: Cotton Plantations and the Formation of Arkansas, 1819–1861* (Fayetteville: Univ. of Arkansas Press, 2000), 100–102.

13. Reported Deaths, *Nashville Christian Advocate,* July–Dec. 1850, comp. Jonathan K. T. Smith, 2003, at *Tennessee Genealogy & History: TNGenWeb Project,* http://www.tngenweb.org/records/tn_wide/obits/nca/nca50-05.htm. (This Web site incorrectly gives Rosa's name as "Rosy.")

14. Ellen Carol DuBois and Lynn Dumenil, *Through Women's Eyes: An American History* (Boston: Bedford/St. Martin's, 2005), 160–61; McCurry, *Masters of Small Worlds,* 56–61, 81–85, 121–26.

15. Sally G. McMillen, *Southern Women: Black and White in the Old South* (Arlington Heights, IL: Harlan Davidson, 1992), 64–79, 86.

16. *Eighth Census, 1860,* Free Schedules, Bolivar County, MS, M653, roll 578; "Mississippi Marriages, 1776–1936," Ancestry.com (subscription-based Web site): http://www.search.ancestry.com.

17. *Eighth Census, 1860,* Free Schedules, Bolivar County, MS, M653, roll 578; *Eighth Census, 1860,* Slave Schedules, Bolivar County, MS, M653, roll 595.

18. Peter Kolchin, *American Slavery, 1619–1877* (New York: Hill and Wang, 1993), 93–105. For slave life on larger plantations, see John Blassingame, *The Slave Community: Plantation Life in the Antebellum South* (New York: Oxford Univ. Press, 1979), 105–93.

19. The rules of paternalism between masters and slaves required subservience from the latter. See Eugene D. Genovese, *Roll, Jordan, Roll: The World the Slaves Made* (New York: Vintage Books, 1974), 90–92.

20. Grover Moore, "Separation from the Union," in *A History of Mississippi*, vol. 1, ed. Richard McLemore, 420–46 (Jackson: Univ. & College Press of Mississippi, 1973).

21. Robert W. Dubay, *John Jones Pettus, Mississippi Fire-Eater: His Life and Times, 1813–1867* (Jackson: Univ. Press of Mississippi, 1975), 21–36. See also Moore, "Separation from the Union,"436.

22. Moore, "Separation from the Union," 436–37.

23. Percy Lee Rainwater, *Mississippi: A Storm Center of Secession, 1856–1861* (Baton Rouge: J. E. Ortlieb Printing Co., 1938), 135–36.

24. David Potter, *The Impending Crisis, 1848–1861* (New York: Harper & Row, 1976), 405–47.

25. Ibid.

26. Dubay, *John Jones Pettus, Mississippi Fire-Eater,* 52–91.

27. Ibid., 99–100. Also see Bobby Roberts and Carl Moneyhon, *Portraits of Conflict: A Photographic History of Mississippi in the Civil War* (Fayetteville: Univ. of Arkansas Press, 1993), 20–21.

28. Richard H. Sewell, *A House Divided: Sectionalism and Civil War, 1848–1865* (Baltimore: Johns Hopkins Univ. Press, 1988), 84–87.

29. Dubay, *John Jones Pettus, Mississippi Fire-Eater,* 106.

30. Ibid., 108.

31. Company A, 20th Mississippi Infantry, Confederate, Company Muster Roll, Aug. 31, 1861 to Aug. 1, 1862, Mississippi Dept. of Archives and History, Jackson.

32. Dunbar Rowland, *Military History of Mississippi, 1803–1898* (Madison: Chickasaw Bayou Press, 2003), 39, 222.

33. Ibid., 222–25, 233–41.

34. Lonnie R. Speer, *Portals to Hell: Military Prisons of the Civil War* (Mechanicsburg, PA: Stackpole Books, 1997), 71–73.

35. For Ignatius Bankston, see Company E, 28th Mississippi Calvary, Confederate, Company Muster Roll, Mar. 10, 1862; for Isaac, see Company D, 28th Mississippi Calvary, Confederate, Company Muster Roll, Mar. 9, 1862. See Mississippi Dept. of Archives and History, Jackson, for both records.

36. Reid Mitchell, *Civil War Soldiers: Their Expectations and Their Experiences* (New York: Simon & Schuster, 1988), 24–28, 63–64, 166–68; Richard Baumgartner, ed., *William Pitt Chambers, Blood and Sacrifice: The Civil War Journal of a Confederate Soldier* (Huntington, WV: Blue Acorn Press, 1994), 75–86. For a more detailed account of company activity during the war, see Janet B. Hewitt, ed., *Supplement to the Official Records of the Union and Confederate Armies,* vol. 33 (Wilmington, NC: Broadfoot Publishing Co., 1996), 517, 536, 671.

37. The last entry for Ignatius Bankston in his company's muster roll was September–October 1862. Also see Kenneth E. French, "Isaac Bankston," *Desha County Historical Society Quarterly 1969–1993* 18, no. 1 (1993): 61–63.

38. There is no record of Isaac Bankston on his company's muster roll for November–December 1862. For William L. Bankston, see Company D, 28th Mississippi Calvary, Confederate, Company Muster Roll, Sept.–Oct., 1863, Mississippi Dept. of Archives and History, Jackson.

39. Company D, 28th Mississippi Calvary, Confederate, Company Muster Roll, Nov.–Dec., 1863, Mississippi Dept. of Archives and History, Jackson.

40. William C. Davis, *Look Away! A History of the Confederate States of America* (New York: Free Press, 2002), 194–224; Amy E. Murrell, "Of Necessity and Public Benefit," in *Southern Families at War: Loyalty*

and Conflict in the Civil War South, ed. Catherine Clinton, 77–99, (New York: Oxford Univ. Press, 2000).

41. Sillers, *History of Bolivar County,* 94–96. See also French, "Isaac Bankston," 62.

42. Katherine Clements Branton and Alice Clements Wade, eds., *Early Mississippi Records: Bolivar County,* vol. 3, *1866–1900* (Jackson: Mississippi Dept. of Archives and History, 1990), 114; French, "Isaac Bankston," 62.

2. The Confluence across the River

1. John William Graves, *Town and Country: Race Relations in an Urban-Rural Context, Arkansas, 1865–1905* (Fayetteville: Univ. of Arkansas Press, 1990), 7, 8.

2. Carl H. Moneyhon, *The Impact of the Civil War and Reconstruction on Arkansas: Persistence in the Midst of Ruin* (Fayetteville: Univ. of Arkansas Press, 2002), 196.

3. Graves, *Town and Country,* 9

4. Ibid., 10.

5. Moneyhon, *The Impact of the Civil War and Reconstruction on Arkansas,* 205–6.

6. Eric Foner, *A Short History of Reconstruction* (New York: Harper & Row, 1990), 104–23.

7. Graves, *Town and Country,* 30–31.

8. Thomas A. DeBlack, *With Fire and Sword: Arkansas, 1861–1874* (Fayetteville: Univ. of Arkansas Press, 2003), 202; Charles F. Robinson, *Dangerous Liaisons: Sex and Love in the Segregated South* (Fayetteville: Univ. of Arkansas Press, 2003), 29.

9. Joseph M. St. Hilaire, "The Negro Delegates in the Constitutional Convention of 1868: A Group Profile," *Arkansas Historical*

Quarterly 33 (Spring 1974): 43–46, 60–64; *Ninth Census, 1870,* Desha County, AR, M593, roll 52. A reference to James Baldwin is found in Charles Patton to I. & M. Bankston, Desha County Records, Deed Records, Book E, 1872, roll 55 (microfilm), Arkansas Historical Commission, Little Rock.

10. *Arkansas Gazette,* Aug. 29, 1876.

11. James Alex Baggett, *The Scalawags: Southern Dissenters in the Civil War and Reconstruction* (Baton Rouge: Louisiana State Univ. Press, 2003), 207–37.

12. Carl H. Moneyhon, "Black Politics in Arkansas During the Gilded Age, 1876–1900," *Arkansas Historical Quarterly* 44 (Autumn 1985): 222–45.

13. Ibid.

14. *Arkansas Gazette,* Aug. 29, 1876.

15. A list of Desha County officeholders is found in *Biographical & Historical Memoirs of Southern Arkansas* (Chicago: Goodspeed Publishing Co., 1890), 998–99. See also *Tenth Census, 1880,* Desha County, AR, T9, roll 43.

16. J. P. and Maime Jones to Isaac & Martha Bankston, Desha County Records, Deed Records, Book 3, 1876–79, roll 56 (microfilm), Arkansas Historical Commission, Little Rock.

17. For examples of the various duties that Isaac performed see Desha County Records, Deed Record Books, 1–2, 3, 4, 5, 1873–85, rolls 55–60 (microfilm), Arkansas Historical Commission, Little Rock. For descriptions of Merritt and McGhee, see *Biographical & Historical Memoirs of Southern Arkansas* (Chicago: Goodspeed Publishing Co., 1890), 1031, 1035. For Henry Thane, see Carolyn Kelley Porter, "Henry Thane," *Programs of the Desha County Historical Society* 19 (Winter 1995):16–27. For the case involving McGehee, see "Isaac Bankston to Benjamin McGehee," Desha County Records, Deed Records, book 4, roll 59 (microfilm), Arkansas Historical Commission, Little Rock.

18. *Arkansas Gazette,* Mar. 11, 17, and 21, 1882.

19. *Tenth Census, 1880,* Desha County, AR, T9, roll 43. For data on the Bankstons' agricultural holdings, I consulted the following U.S. census record preserved on microfilm at the Mullins Library, Univ. of Arkansas, Fayetteville: Census, 1880, Arkansas, Agriculture, Jefferson Township, Desha County, AR, reel 1, p. 9.

20. *Arkansas City Journal,* Dec. 23, 1882.

21. *Tenth Census, 1880,* Bolivar County, MS, T9, roll 641.

22. Vernon Lane Wharton, *The Negro in Mississippi, 1865–1890* (New York: Harper & Row, 1965), 18–48.

23. Ibid., 85.

24. Ibid., 84.

25. "Memphis Riot and Massacres" (U.S. Document 1274, 39th Congress, 1st sess., 1865–66, House Reports, vol. 3, no. 101), excerpted in *Black Women in White America: A Documentary History,* ed. Gerda Lerner, 172–77 (New York: Vintage Books, 1992).

26. Ibid.

27. Stanley F. Horn, *Invisible Empire: The Story of the Ku Klux Klan, 1866–1871* (Montclair, NJ: Patterson Smith, 1969), 7–20, 145–67.

28. George Rawick, ed., *The American Slave: A Composite Autobiography,* supp., ser. 1, vol. 6, *Mississippi Narratives,* pt. 1 (Westport, CT: Greenwood Publishing, 1977): 255–61.

29. Rawick, *American Slave,* supp., ser. 1, vol. 7, *Mississippi Narratives,* pt. 2: 525–28.

30. Jaqueline Jones, *Labor of Love, Labor of Sorrow: Black Women, Work, and the Family from Slavery to the Present* (New York: Basic Books, 1985), 60–65; Nancy Bercaw, *Gendered Freedoms: Race, Rights, and the Politics of Household in the Delta, 1861–1875* (Gainsville: Univ. Press of Florida, 2003), 99–116; Laura F. Edwards, *Gendered Strife and Confusion: The Political Culture of Reconstruction* (Urbana: Univ. of Illinois Press, 1997), 143–83.

31. Jones, *Labor of Love, Labor of Sorrow,* 68–72.

32. Wharton, *Negro in Mississippi,* 243–55.

33. Jones, *Labor of Love, Labor of Sorrow,* 76.

34. *Tenth Census, 1880,* Bolivar County, MS, T9, roll 641.

35. Ibid.

36. Jones, *Labor of Love, Labor of Sorrow,* 113.

37. L. A. Emerson, "History of Railroads in Arkansas and Desha County," *Programs of the Desha County Historical Society* 5 (1978): 23–27; Merritt, "Arkansas City," 13–17.

38. *Arkansas City Journal,* Dec. 23, 1882; Aug. 15, 1883.

39. *Arkansas Gazette,* Jan. 1, Mar. 18, and May 31, 1881; Feb. 22 and Apr. 20, 1882.

40. Clipping, WPA file, Arkansas County Histories Collection, 1936–1941, Desha County, Part IV (microfilm), Arkansas Historical Commission, Little Rock.

41. E. M. Dreidel, "Desha County Court House at Arkansas City: The First Court House, Arkansas City," *Programs of the Desha County Historical Society* 1 (1975): 19–22.

42. *Arkansas Gazette,* Feb. 12, 1884. Missouri mentioned in one *Gazette* article that she had met Isaac sometime in 1881. This suggests that she probably moved to Arkansas City around that time.

3. In Search of Their Place

1. Martha Hodes, *White Women, Black Men: Illicit Love in the Nineteenth Century South* (New Haven, CT: Yale Univ. Press, 1997), 1–4.

2. *Campbell v. Campbell,* 13 Ark. 573 (1845).

3. *Moss v. Sandefur,* 15 Ark. 381 (1847).

4. David B. Quinn, *The Elizabethans and the Irish* (Ithaca, NY: Cornell Univ. Press, 1966), 64, 70, 81–83; Reay Tannahill, *Sex in History* (New York: Scarborough House, 1992), 315–18; Winthrop D. Jordan, *White over Black: American Attitudes toward the Negro, 1550–1812* (New York: W. W. Norton, 1968), 32–40.

5. Kathleen M. Brown, *Good Wives, Nasty Wenches, and Anxious Patriarchs: Gender, Race, and Power in Colonial Virginia* (Chapel Hill: Univ. of North Carolina Press, 1985), 13–41; James H. Johnston, *Race Relations in Virginia and Miscegenation in the South, 1776–1860* (Amherst: Univ. of Massachusetts Press, 1970), 167.

6. Peter W. Bardaglio, "Shameful Matches," in *Sex, Love, Race: Crossing Boundaries in Northern American History,* ed. Martha Hodes, 115 (New York: Peter Lang, 1993); John D. Emilio and Estelle B. Freedman, *Intimate Matters: A History of Sexuality in America,* 2nd ed. (Chicago: Univ. of Chicago Press, 1997), 10, 37.

7. A. Leon Higginbotham Jr. and Barbara Kopytoff, "Racial Purity and Interracial Sex in the Law of Colonial and Antebellum Virginia," in *Interracialism: Black-White Intermarriage in American History, Literature, and Law,* ed. Werner Sollors, 45–46 (New York: Oxford Univ. Press, 2000); David Fowler, *Northern Attitudes towards Interracial Marriage: Legislation and Public Opinion in Middle Atlantic States of the Old Northwest, 1780–1930* (New York: Garland Publishing, 1987), 56–61; Lorenzo J. Greene, *The Negro in Colonial New England* (New York: Atheneum, 1969), 208.

8. Joshua Rothman, *Notorious In The Neighborhood: Sex and Families Across the Color Line in Virginia, 1787–1861* (Chapel Hill: Univ. of North Carolina Press, 2003), 56–87; 171–72.

9. *Bonds v. Foster,* 36 Tex. 68; *Honey v. Clark,* 37 Tex. 686 (1872).

10. Robinson, *Dangerous Liaisons,* 21–40.

11. Charles Robinson, "'Most Shamefully Common': Arkansas and Miscegenation," *Arkansas Historical Quarterly* 55 (Fall 2001): 272–74; *Ninth Census, 1870,* Pulaski County, AR, M593, roll 62; *Tenth Census, 1880,* Pulaski County, AR, T9, rolls 54–55; Kelley Metheny, "Interracial Marriage and Cohabitation in Pulaski County, Arkansas, 1870–1900," *Pulaski County Historical Review,* 44 (Summer 1996): 30–42.

12. J. N. Cypert of White County, AR, quoted in Peter W. Bardaglio, *Reconstructing the Household: Families, Sex, and Law in the Nineteenth-Century South* (Chapel Hill: Univ. of North Carolina Press, 1995), 177.

See also Paul C. Palmer, "Miscegenation as an Issue in the Arkansas Constitutional Convention of 1868," *Arkansas Historical Quarterly* 24 (Spring–Winter 1965): 99–119.

13. *Scott v. State,* 39 Ga. 321 (1869); *State v. Bell,* 66 Tenn. 9 (1872).

14. Robinson, *Dangerous Liaisons,* 41–59.

15. Ibid., 49–56.

16. Bertram Wyatt-Brown, *Honor and Violence in the Old South* (New York: Oxford Univ. Press, 1986), 95–98, 105–8.

17. Herbert G. Gutman, *The Black Family in Slavery and Freedom, 1750–1925* (New York: Vintage Books, 1976), 67–70, 74–75.

18. *Arkansas Gazette,* Feb. 8, 1880. Also see Elizabeth Gilmore, *Gender and Jim Crow: Women and the Politics of White Supremacy in North Carolina, 1896–1920* (Chapel Hill: Univ. of North Carolina Press, 1996), 70–71.

19. Robinson, *Dangerous Liaisons,* 114–28.

20. On the importance of maintaining the surreptitious nature of interracial relationships, see Wyatt-Brown, *Honor and Violence in the Old South,* 105–6.

21. Robinson, *Dangerous Liaisons,* 87–88.

22. Marriage License for Isaac Bankston and Missouri Bradford, Marriage Book K, Dec. 29, 1883, p. 372, Shelby County Archives, Memphis, TN.

23. *Arkansas Gazette,* Feb. 12, 1884.

24. *Arkansas Gazette,* June 3, 1884.

25. Robinson, *Dangerous Liaisons,* 88–94.

26. Tera Hunter, *To 'Joy My Freedom: Southern Black Women's Lives and Labors After the Civil War* (Cambridge: Harvard Univ. Press, 1998), 52, 107–14.

27. *Arkansas Gazette,* Feb. 12, 1884.

28. *Tenth Census, 1880,* Bolivar County, MS, T9, rolls 641–42; *Arkansas Gazette,* Feb. 12, 1884.

29. *Bonds v. Foster,* 36 Tex. 68 (1870).

30. *Kinard v. State,* 57 Miss. 132 (1879).

31. John D'Emilio and Estelle B. Freedman, *Intimate Matters: A History of Sexuality in America 2nd Ed.* (Chicago: Univ. of Chicago Press, 1997), 97, 98.

32. *Arkansas Gazette,* Dec. 21 and Dec. 22, 1883.

33. *Arkansas Gazette,* Aug. 4, 1883.

34. *Arkansas Gazette,* Sept. 12, 1883.

35. Ibid.

36. *Arkansas Gazette,* Dec. 21, 1883.

37. *Arkansas Gazette,* Dec. 23, 1883.

38. *Arkansas Gazette,* Jan. 11, 1884.

39. Ibid.

4. From Memphis to Marriage and Misery

1. *Sholes' Memphis City Directory* (Atlanta: A. E. Sholes and Co.), 1883, 1884.

2. *Memphis Daily Appeal,* Mar. 20 and May 8, 1884.

3. *Memphis Daily Appeal,* Mar. 13, 1884.

4. *Sholes' Memphis City Directory,* 1884.

5. Christopher Caplinger, "Conflict and Community: Racial Segregation in a New South City, 1860–1914" (PhD diss., Dept. of History, Vanderbilt Univ.), 2003, 18.

6. Ibid., 23.

7. Ibid., 24; Kathleen Christine Berkeley, "'Like a Plague of Locusts': Immigration and Social Change in Memphis, Tennessee, 1850–1880," PhD diss., Dept. of History, Univ. of California, 1980, 149.

8. Denoral Davis, "Against the Odds: Postbellum Growth and Development in a Southern Black Urban Community, 1865–1900" (PhD diss., Dept. of History, State Univ. of New York at Binghamton, 1987), 106–8.

9. Berkeley, "'Like a Plague of Locust,'" 173–75; Armstead L. Robinson, "Plans Dat Comed from God: Institution Building and the Emergence of Black Leadership in Reconstruction Memphis," in *Toward A New South? Studies in Post–Civil War Southern Communities,* ed. Orville Vernon Burton and Robert C. McMath Jr., 79–80 (Westport: Greenwood Press, 1982).

10. Berkeley, "'Like a Plague of Locusts,'" 175–76.

11. *Sholes' Memphis City Directory,* 1884

12. Caplinger, "Conflict and Community," 58.

13. Dennis C. Rousey, "Yellow Fever and Black Policemen in Memphis: A Post-Reconstruction Anomaly," *Journal of Southern History* 51 (Aug. 1985): 357–74.

14. Caplinger, "Conflict and Community," 43.

15. *Sholes' Memphis City Directory,* 1884.

16. Carole M. Ornelas-Struve and Joan Hassell, eds., *Memphis: Years of Courage, 1870–1900,* vol. 3 (New York: Nancy Powers & Co., 1982), 30.

17. *Memphis Daily Appeal,* May 20, 1884.

18. *Memphis: Years of Courage, 1870–1900,* 31; Davis, "Against the odds," 206–43.

19. Joseph H. Cartwright, *The Triumph of Jim Crow: Tennessee Race Relations in the 1880s* (Knoxville: Univ. of Tennessee Press, 1976), 175–76.

20. Alfreda M. Duster, ed. *Crusade for Justice: The Autobiography of Ida B. Wells* (Chicago: Univ. of Chicago Press, 1970), 18, 19.

21. Duster, *Crusade for Justice,* 19, 20; *The Memphis Appeal-Avalanche,* Dec. 25, 1884; *Chesapeake & Ohio & Southwestern Railroad Company v. Wells,* 85 Tennessee Reports 613 (1885).

22. *Memphis Daily Appeal,* May 20, 1884.

23. *Memphis Daily Appeal,* May 13, 1884.

24. Howard Rabinowitz, *Race Relations in the Urban South, 1865–1890* (New York: Oxford Univ. Press, 1978), x, xi; 127–97.

25. *Arkansas Gazette,* Nov. 6, 1883; Nov. 9, 1883.

26. *Arkansas Gazette,* Nov. 6, 1883; Nov. 7, 1883.

27. *Tenth Census, 1880,* Shelby County, TN, T9, roll 1279; *Sholes' Memphis City Directory,* 1884.

28. *Tenth Census, 1880,* Shelby County, TN, T9, roll 1279.

29. *Arkansas Gazette,* Feb. 12, 1884.

30. Ibid.

31. Ibid.

32. *Goodspeed's History of Hamilton, Knox and Shelby Counties of Tennessee* (Nashville: Charles and Randy Elder Booksellers, 1887), 947; *Memphis As She Is: Rambles in the Path of Industrial & Commercial Circles* (Memphis: Historical and Descriptive Publishing Company, 1887), 98.

33. *Tenth Census, 1880,* Shelby County, TN, T9, roll 1279; *Sholes' Memphis City Directory,* 1884.

34. Marriage License, Isaac Bankston and Missouri Bradford.

35. "Banns, Marriage Bonds and Licenses, and Bastardy Bonds," comp. Fred Smoot at *Tennessee Genealogy & History: TNGenWeb Project,* http://www.tngenweb.org/law/bond.htm.

36. Marriage License, Isaac Bankston and Missouri Bradford.

37. Secs. 2425, 2437, 2445, 2446, 2447, 4924, 4925, 4926, 4927 (1857–58), in *The Code of Tennessee: Enacted by the General Assembly*

of 1857–'8, ed. Return J. Meigs and William F. Cooper (Nashville: E. G. Eastman & Co., 1858).

38. *Memphis Daily Appeal,* Dec. 30, 1883.

39. *Arkansas Gazette,* Jan. 9, 1884.

40. *Arkansas Democrat,* Jan. 10, 1884

41. *Arkansas Gazette,* Jan. 10, 1884.

42. *Arkansas Gazette,* Jan. 11, 1884.

43. A number of secondary works elaborate on white perceptions of black women as seductresses. See Stephanie M. H. Camp, *Closer to Freedom: Enslaved Women and Everyday Resistance in the Plantation South* (Chapel Hill: Univ. of North Carolina Press, 2004), 63–65; Hunter, *To 'Joy My Freedom,* 106–7, 166, 179–81; and Noralee Frankel, *Freedom's Women: Black Women and Families in Civil War Era Mississippi* (Bloomington: Indiana Univ. Press, 1999), 116–21.

44. *Arkansas Gazette,* Feb. 6, 1884.

45. Ibid.

46. Ibid.

47. *Arkansas Gazette,* Feb. 12, 1884.

48. *Arkansas Gazette,* Feb. 19, 1884.

49. *Arkansas Gazette,* Mar. 4, 1884.

50. *Memphis Daily Appeal,* Feb. 17, 1884; Marriage License for James Chambers and Nannie Bennett, Marriage Book K, July 7, 1883, p. 247, Shelby County Archives, Memphis, TN.

51. *State of Tennessee v. Isaac Bankston & Missouri Bradford,* indictment for illegal cohabitation, Criminal Court Clerk, Reel 14, Division 1, Minute Book 44, pp. 119–21, Shelby County Archive, Memphis, TN. With regard to the marriage license, Isaac must have returned it to the clerk's office. He probably did so by mail rather than in person. There is no record that he actually returned to the city.

52. *Arkansas Gazette,* May 5, 1884.

5. Color Line Justice

1. "An Act Concerning Servants and Slaves" (1741), reprinted in *The State Records of North Carolina (1777–1790),* ed. Walter Clark, vol. 23: 160 (Greensboro: Nash Brothers, 1886–1907).

2. "An Act to Amend the Law Concerning Marriage" (1822), ch. 19, *Acts of a General Public Nature Passed at the Second Session of the Fourteenth General Assembly of Tennessee,* 22–23 (Knoxville: Herskell & Brown, 1822).

3. Robinson, *Dangerous Liaisons,* 1–5, 71.

4. *Richmond v. Richmond,* 18 Tenn. 342 (1837).

5. *State v. Brady,* 28 Tenn. 74 (1848).

6. Legal authorities throughout the nation generally imposed antimiscegenation laws more heavily against white women. See Peter W. Bardaglio, "Shameful Matches," in *Sex, Love, Race: Crossing Boundaries in North American History,* ed. Martha Hodes, 115 (New York: New York Univ. Press, 1999).

7. *Bloomer v. State,* 35 Tenn. 66 (1855).

8. "An Act providing for the voluntary enslavement of free persons of color in this state" (1858), ch. 45, secs. 1, 2, 4, and 6, in *Public Acts of the State of Tennessee, 1857–1858* (Nashville: G. C. Torbett & Co., 1858).

9. Secs. 2425, 2437, 2445, 2446, 2447, 4924, 4925, 4926, 4927 (1857–58), in *The Code of Tennessee, 1857–1858,* ed. Returns J. Meigs and William F. Cooper (Nashville: E. G. Eastman & Co., 1858).

10. *Ford v. Ford,* 26 Tenn. 91 (1846).

11. Joseph H. Cartwright, *The Triumph of Jim Crow: Tennessee Race Relations in the 1880s* (Knoxville: Univ. of Tennessee Press, 1981), 8–11.

12. Cartwright, *The Triumph of Jim Crow,* 8–11.

13. See Alrutheus A. Taylor, *The Negro in Tennessee, 1865–1880* (Washington, D.C.: Association for Study of Negro Life and History,

1941), 228–29, for summaries of the *Nation* (July 19, 1866) and *Nashville Republican Banner* (Aug. 18, 1866) reportage.

14. In *The Code of Tennessee . . . 1884,* ed. W. A. Milliken and John J. Vertrees, xcix (Nashville: Marshall & Bruce, 1884).

15. "An Act to Enforce Section 14, Article 11 of the Constitution, and to Prevent Intermarriage of White Persons with Negroes, Mulattoes or Persons of Mixed Blood" (1870), ch. 39, *Acts of the State of Tennessee, Second Session, 1869–70,* 69–70 (Nashville: Jones, Purvis & Co., 1870).

16. *James & Mollie Robertson v. State,* 50 Tenn. 266 (1871).

17. *Lonas v. State,* 50 Tenn. 287 (1871).

18. Ibid.

19. *State v. Bell,* 66 Tenn. 9 (1872).

20. Shelby County Criminal Court, Minute Book 44, div. 1, pp. 79–81, Shelby County Archives, Memphis, TN.

21. Jail Reports, Jan. 1880–Nov. 1887, Shelby County Archives, Memphis, TN.

22. *Arkansas Gazette,* May 11, 1884.

23. *Memphis Daily Appeal,* May 11, 1884.

24. *Memphis Public Ledger,* May 22, 1884.

25. *Sholes' Memphis City Directory,* 1884. See also *Tenth Census, 1880,* District 4, Benton County, TN, T9, roll 1244.

26. John B. Getz and Joe Walk, comps. and eds., "History of the District Attorney General's Office and the Public Defender's Office of Shelby County Tennessee," 2003, unpublished paper, Shelby County Archives, Memphis, TN.

27. *Memphis Daily Appeal,* May 13 and 28, 1884.

28. *Moore v. State,* 7 Tex. 608 (1880).

29. *McPherson v. Commonwealth,* 69 Va. 939 (1877).

30. *Jones v. Commonwealth,* 79 Va. 213 (1884).

31. Other works have documented incidences of passing. See Willard B. Gatewood Jr., "The Perils of Passing: The McCrarys of Omaha," *Nebraska History* 71 (Summer 1990): 64–70; and Willard B. Gatewood Jr., *Aristocrats of Color: The Black Elite, 1880–1920* (Fayetteville: Univ. of Arkansas, 2000), 170–72.

32. Richard White, *The Middle Ground: Indian, Empires, and Republics in the Great Lake Region, 1650–1815* (New York: Cambridge Univ. Press, 1991), 33.

33. Joel W. Martin, "'My Grandmother Was A Cherokee Princess': Representations of Indians in Southern History," in *Dressing in Feathers: The Construction of the Indian in American Popular Culture,* ed. S. Elizabeth Bird, 130–41 (Boulder: Westview Press, 1996).

34. Ibid.

35. D'Emilio and Freedman, *Intimate Matters,* 10, 37.

36. Martin, "'My Grandmother Was A Cherokee Princess,'" 132–34.

37. Ibid., 134–35.

38. Laura L. Lovett, "'Africans and Cherokee by Choice': Race and Resistance under Legalized Segregation," in *Confounding the Color Line: The Indian-Black Experience in North America,* ed. James F. Brooks, 192–222 (Lincoln: Univ. of Nebraska Press, 2002).

39. Shelby County Criminal Court, Minute Book 45, div. 1, pp. 76–68, Shelby County Archives, Memphis, TN; *Sholes' Memphis City Directory,* 1883. I also found Henry Hoss in the *Thirteenth Census, 1910,* Shelby County, TN, T624, roll 1518.

40. Shelby County Criminal Court, Execution Docket, May Term, 1884, Shelby County Archives, Memphis, TN.

41. *Arkansas Gazette,* June 1, 1884.

42. Shelby County Criminal Court, Minute Book 45, div. 1, pp. 67–68, Shelby County Archives, Memphis, TN.

43. Ibid.

44. Robert A. Lanier, *The History of the Memphis and Shelby County Bar* ([Memphis?]: n.p., 1981), 42, 43, 53.

45. John B. Getz and Joe Walk, "History of the District Attorney General's Office and the Public Defender's Office of Shelby County, Tennessee," unpublished paper, 26–27, Shelby County Archives, Memphis, TN.

46. *Walls v. State,* 32 Ark. 565 (1877); *Scroggins v. State,* 32, Ark. 205 (1877).

47. Milliken and Vertrees, *Code of Tennessee . . . 1884,* Art. 2, Secs. 5649, 5650, 5651, 5652.

6. A Quest for Honor

1. *Memphis Daily Appeal,* June 1, 1884.

2. W. J. Cash, *The Mind of the South* (New York: Alfred A. Knopf, 1941), 42–44.

3. John Hope Franklin, *The Militant South* (Cambridge: Harvard Univ. Press, 1956), 33–61; Bertram Wyatt-Brown, *The Shaping of Southern Culture: Honor, Grace, and War, 1760s–1880s* (Chapel Hill: Univ. of North Carolina Press, 2001), 52; Wyatt-Brown, *Honor and Violence in the Old South,* 154–86.

4. Dickson D. Bruce Jr., *Violence and Culture in the Antebellum South* (Austin: Univ. of Texas Press, 1979), 8–12.

5. Wyatt-Brown, *Honor and Violence in the Old South,* vii, viii.

6. Ibid., viii, 63–64.

7. McMillen, *Southern Women,* 9, 79, 84.

8. D'Emilio and Freedman, *Intimate Matters,* 95–96; Wyatt-Brown, *Honor and Violence in the Old South,* 95–105.

9. Cash, *The Mind of the South,* 113–17.

10. Edward L. Ayers, *Vengeance and Justice: Crime and Punishment in the 19th Century American South* (New York: Oxford Univ. Press, 1884), 238–53.

11. *Arkansas Gazette,* July 19, 1881.

12. *Arkansas Gazette,* July 28, 1882.

13. *Marshall–Tri Weekly Herald,* Dec. 2, 1879.

14. *Arkansas Gazette,* Mar. 20, 1881.

15. *Arkansas Gazette,* Sept. 21, 1886.

16. *Memphis Daily Appeal,* Apr. 26, 1884.

17. Wyatt-Brown, *The Shape of Southern Culture,* 3–27; D'Emilio and Freedman, *Intimate Matters,* 104–5.

18. See Catherine Clinton, "Bloody Terrain: Freedwomen, Sexuality and Violence during Reconstruction" in *Half Sisters of History: Southern Women and the American Past,* ed. Catherine Clinton (Durham: Duke Univ. Press, 1994), 42.

19. Ayers, *Vengeance and Justice,* 233–35.

20. *Arkansas Gazette,* Dec. 29, 1882.

21. *Arkansas Gazette,* July 25, 1885.

22. *Arkansas Gazette,* June 3, 1884.

23. Ibid.

24. Jack Williams, *Dueling in the Old South* (College Station, Texas A&M Univ. Press, 1980), 26–39.

25. *Arkansas Gazette,* June 3, 1884; *Memphis Daily Appeal,* June 7, 1884.

26. *Arkansas Gazette,* June 5, 1880.

27. Desha County Records, Probate Records, Arkansas Historical Commission, Little Rock.

28. *Arkansas Gazette,* June 5, 1880.

29. Shelby County Criminal Court, Minute Book 45, div. 1, p. 73, Shelby County Archives, Memphis, TN.

30. Desha County Records, Probate Records, Arkansas Historical Commission, Little Rock.

31. Tillar Hutchens Landfair, "Life and Times of Sheriff Bill Preston," *Programs of the Desha County Historical Society* 1 (1974): 37–42.

32. *Twelfth Census, 1900,* Desha County, AR, T623, roll 57. In his biographical article "Isaac Bankston," Kenneth French mentions that Martha died in 1905 (p. 63).

33. *Fourteenth Census, 1920,* Desha County, AR, T625, roll 61.

34. *Fifteenth Census, 1930,* Desha County, AR, T626, roll 73.

Conclusion

1. See Wyatt-Brown, *Honor and Violence in the Old South;* Cash, *The Mind of the South;* and Robinson, *Dangerous Liaisons.*

2. See Jones, *Labor of Love, Labor of Sorrow;* and Hunter, *To 'Joy My Freedom.*

3. See Elizabeth Fox-Genovese, *Within the Plantation Household: Black and White Women of the Old South* (Chapel Hill: Univ. of North Carolina Press, 1988); and Bardaglio, *Reconstructing the Household.*

4. See Victoria Bynum, "'White Negroes' in Segregated Mississippi: Miscegenation, Racial Identity, and the Law," *Journal of Southern History* 114 (May1998): 247–76; and Gatewood, "The Perils of Passing," 64–70.

5. Robinson, *Dangerous Liaisons,* 114–32.

6. U.S. Bureau of the Census, "Families and Living Arrangements: Marital Status, Table MS-3 (Interacial Married Couples, 1980–2002)," http://www.census.gov/population/www/socdemo/hh-fam.xls.

7. "Louisiana Newlyweds Want Justice of Peace Fired," *CNN.com/ US,* Oct. 19, 2009, http://www.cnn.com/2009/US/10/19/interracial. marriage/index.html.

BIBLIOGRAPHY

Primary Sources

ARCHIVAL DOCUMENTS

Arkansas Historical Commission, Little Rock.
> Desha County Records, Deed Records. Book E, 1872;
>> Books 1–5, 1873–1885. Microfilm.
>
> WPA File, Arkansas County Histories Collection,
>> 1936–1941. Desha County, Part IV. Microfilm.
>
> Desha County Records, Probate Records: Estate Settle-
>> ments, 1857–1899, Rolls 31, 32. Microfilm.

Mississippi Department of Archives and History, Jackson.
> Company A, 20th Mississippi Infantry, Confederate,
>> Company Muster Roll, William Bankston,
>> August 31, 1861 to August 1, 1862. Microfilm.
>
> Company D, 28th Mississippi Calvary, Confederate,
>> Company Muster Roll, William L. Bankston,
>> September–October, 1863. Microfilm.
>
> Company E, 28th Mississippi Calvary, Confederate,
>> Company Muster Roll, Ignatius Bankston,
>> March 10, 1862. Microfilm.
>
> Company D, Mississippi Calvary, Confederate, Company
>> Muster Roll, Isaac Bankston, March 9, 1862,
>> September–October, 1863; November–Decem-
>> ber, 1863. Microfilm.

Shelby County Archives, Memphis, TN.

Execution Docket, Shelby County Criminal Court, May Term, 1884.

Getz, John B., and Joe Walk, comps. and eds. "History of the District Attorney General's Office and the Public Defender's Office of Shelby County, Tennessee." Unpublished paper.

Grand Jury Docket, Shelby County Criminal Court, 1884.

Jail Reports, January 1880–November 1887.

Marriage License for Isaac Bankston and Missouri Bradford. Marriage Book K, p. 372, December 29, 1883.

Marriage License for James Chambers and Nannie Bennett. Marriage Book K, July 7, p. 247, 1883.

State of Tennessee v. Isaac Bankston & Missouri Bradford. Shelby County Criminal Court, Minute Books 44 and 45.

Books

Biographical & Historical Memoirs of Southern Arkansas. Chicago: Goodspeed Publishing Co., 1890.

Branton, Katherine C., and Alice C. Wade. *Early Mississippi Records: Bolivar County.* Vol. 1, *1836–1861.* Jackson: Mississippi Department of Archives and History, 1988.

———. *Early Mississippi Records: Bolivar County.* Vol. 3, *1866–1900.* Jackson: Mississippi Department of Archives and History, 1990.

Goodspeed's History of Hamilton, Knox and Shelby Counties of Tennessee. Nashville: Charles and Randy Elder Booksellers, 1887.

Memphis As She Is: Rambles in the Path of Industrial & Commercial Circles, 1880. Memphis: Historical and Descriptive Publishing Company, 1887.

Sholes' Memphis City Directory. Atlanta: A. E. Sholes and Co., 1883, 1884.

CENSUS RECORDS

All of the official U.S. census records listed below in chronological order have been published on microfilm by the National Archives and Records Administration, Washington, DC. The publication and roll numbers (for example, M19, roll 5) are given with each entry. *Note:* One exception to the use of NARA-published records was the following U.S. census record preserved on microfilm at the Mullins Library, University of Arkansas, Fayetteville: Census, 1880. Arkansas, Agriculture, Jefferson Township, Desha County, AR. Reel 1, page 9.

U.S. Bureau of the Census, *Fifth Census of the United States, 1830.* Population Schedules, Chicot County, Territory of Arkansas. M19, roll 5.

———. *Sixth Census of the United States, 1840.* Population Schedules, Bolivar County, MS. M704, roll 215.

———. *Seventh Census of the United States, 1850.* Free Population Schedules, Bolivar County, MS. M432, roll 368.

———. *Eighth Census of the United States, 1860.* Free Population Schedules, Bolivar County, MS. M653, roll 578.

——. *Eighth Census of the United States, 1860.* Slave Population Schedules, Bolivar County, MS. M653, roll 595.

——. *Ninth Census of the United States, 1870.* Population Schedules, Desha County, AR. M593, roll 52.

——. *Ninth Census of the United States, 1870.* Population Schedules, Pulaski County, AR. M593, roll 62.

——. *Tenth Census of the United States, 1880.* Population Schedules, Desha County, AR. T9, rolls 42–43.

——. *Tenth Census of the United States, 1880.* Population Schedules, Bolivar County, MS. T9, rolls 641–42.

——. *Tenth Census of the United States, 1880.* Population Schedules, District 4, Benton County, TN, T9, roll 1244.

——. *Tenth Census of the United States, 1880.* Population Schedules, Shelby County, TN. T9, rolls 1278–80.

——. *Twelfth Census of the United States, 1900.* Population Schedules, Desha County, AR. T623, roll 57.

——. *Thirteenth Census of the United States, 1910.* Population Schedules, Shelby County, TN. T624, rolls 1519–21.

——. *Fourteenth Census of the United States, 1920.* Population Schedules, Desha County, AR. T625, roll 61.

——. *Fifteenth Census of the United States, 1930.* Population Schedules, Desha County, AR. T626, roll 73.

GOVERNMENT REPORT

"Memphis Riot and Massacres" (U.S. Document 1274, 39th Congress, 1st sess., 1865–66, House Reports, vol.

3, no. 101). Excerpted in *Black Women in White America: A Documentary History,* edited by Gerda Lerner, 172–77. New York: Vintage Books, 1992.

LAWS

"An Act Concerning Servants and Slaves" (1741). Reprinted in *The State Records of North Carolina (1777–1790),* edited by Walter Clark, vol. 23: 160. Greensboro: Nash Brothers, 1886–1907.

"An Act Providing for the Voluntary Enslavement of Free Persons of Color in This State" (1858). Chapter 45, sections 1, 2, 4, 6, *Public Acts of the State of Tennessee, 1857–1858.* Nashville: G. C. Torbett & Co., 1858.

"An Act to Amend the Law Concerning Marriage" (1822). Chapter 19, *Acts of a General public Nature Passed at the Second Session of the Fourteenth General Assembly of Tennessee.* Knoxville: Herskell & Brown, 1822.

"An Act to Enforce Section 14, Article 11 of the Constitution, and to Prevent Intermarriage of White Persons with Negroes, Mulattoes or Persons of Mixed Blood" (1870). Chapter 39, *Acts of the State of Tennessee, Second Session, 1869–70.* Nashville: Jones, Purvis & Co., 1870.

Constitution of Tennessee, Article 11, Section 14 (1870). In *The Code of Tennessee, Being a Compilation of the Statute Laws of the State of Tennessee, of a General Nature, in Force June 1, 1884,* edited by W. A. Milliken and John J. Vertrees, xcix. Nashville: Marshall & Bruce, 1884.

Sections 2425, 2437, 2445, 2446, 2447, 4924, 4925, 4926, 4927
(1857–58). In *The Code of Tennessee: Enacted by
the General Assembly of 1857–'8,* edited by Return
J. Meigs and William F. Cooper. Nashville: E. G.
Eastman & Co., 1858.

LEGAL CASES

Campbell v. Campbell, 13 Ark. 573 (1845).

Moss v. Sandefur, 15 Ark. 381 (1847).

Bonds v. Foster, 36 Tex. 68 (1870).

Honey v. Clark, 37 Tex. 686 (1872).

Scott v. State, 39 Ga. 321 (1869).

Pace & Cox v. State, 69 Ala. 231 (1881).

Pace v. Alabama, 106 U.S. 583 (1883).

Kinard v. State, 57 Miss. 132 (1879).

Richmond v. Richmond, 18 Tenn. 342 (1837).

State v. Brady, 28 Tenn. 74 (1848).

Bloomer v. State, 35 Tenn. 66 (1855).

Ford v. Ford, 26 Tenn. 94 (1846).

James & Mollie Robertson v. State, 50 Tenn. 266 (1871).

Lonas v. State, 50 Tenn. 287 (1871).

State v. Bell, 66 Tenn. 9 (1872).

McPherson v. Commonwealth, 69 Va. 939 (1877).

Jones v. Commonwealth, 79 Va. 213 (1884).

NEWSPAPERS

Arkansas City Journal

Arkansas Democrat

Arkansas Gazette

Memphis Daily Appeal

Memphis Public Ledger

Marshall–Tri Weekly Herald

ONLINE SOURCES

"Mississippi Marriages, 1776–1936." Ancestry.com (subscription-based Web site). http://www.search. ancestry.com.

Tennessee Genealogy and History (TNGenWeb Project). "Banns, Marriage Bonds and Licenses, and Bastardy Bonds." Compiled by Fred Smoot. http:// www.tngenweb.org/law/bond.htm.

———. "Reported Deaths," *Nashville Christian Advocate,* July–Dec. 1850. Compiled by Jonathan K. T. Smith, 2003. http://www.tngenweb.org/records/tn_wide/ obits/nca/nca1-01.htm.

U.S. Bureau of the Census. "Families and Living Arrangements: Marital Status, Table MS-3 (Interracial Married Couples, 1980–2002)." http://www.census. gov/population/www/socdemo/hh-fam.xls.

Secondary Sources

ARTICLES

Baker, Susan E. "Depraved and Abandoned Women: Prostitution in Richmond, Virginia Across the Civil War." In *Neither Lady Nor Slave: Working Women of the Old South,* edited by Susanna Delfina and Michele Gillespie, 155–73. Chapel Hill: The University of North Carolina Press, 2002.

Bardaglio, Peter W. "Shameful Matches." In *Sex, Love, Race: Crossing Boundaries in Northern American History,* edited by Martha Hodes, 112–40. New York: Peter Lang, 1993.

Boerkout, Brock A. and Hendrick, Susan S. "Relationship Infidelity: A Loss Perspective." *Journal of Personal & Interpersonal Loss* 4 (April–June 1999): 97–123.

Buunk, Bram P., and Pieternel Dijkstra. "Men, Women, and Infidelity: Sex Differences in Extradyadic Sex." In *The State of Affairs: Explorations in Infidelity and Commitment,* edited by Jean Duncombe, Kaeren Harrison, Graham Allen, and Dennis Marsden, 103–20. Mahwah, NJ: Lawrence Erilbaum Associates, 2004.

Bynum, Victoria. "'White Negroes' in Segregated Mississippi: Miscegenation, Racial Identity, and the Law." *Journal of Southern History* 114 (May 1998): 247–76.

Clifton, Ann D., "A Demographic Study of Bolivar County in 1860." *Journal of the Bolivar County Historical Society* 1 (March 1977): 10–20.

Clinton, Catherine. "Bloody Terrain: Freedwomen, Sexuality and Violence during Reconstruction. In *Half Sisters of History: Southern Women and the American Past,* edited by Catherine Clinton, 136–53. Durham: Duke University Press, 1994.

Criss, Gail, and Charlotte Hill. "A Demographic Study of Bolivar County in 1850." *Journal of the Bolivar County Historical Society* 1 (March 1977): 3–9.

Dreidel, E. M. "Desha County Court House at Arkansas City: The First Courthouse, Arkansas City." *Programs of the Desha County Historical Society* 1 (1975): 19–22.

Emerson, L. A. "History of Railroads in Arkansas and Desha County." *Programs of the Desha County Historical Society* 5 (1978): 23–27

French, Kenneth E. "Isaac Bankston." *Programs of the Desha County Historical Society* 18 (1993): 61–63.

Gatewood, Willard B. "The Arkansas Delta: The Deepest of the Deep South." In *The Arkansas Delta: Land of Paradox,* edited by Jeannie Whayne and Willard B. Gatewood, 3–29. Fayetteville: University of Arkansas Press, 1993.

———. "The Perils of Passing: The McCrarys of Omaha." *Nebraska History* (Summer 1990): 64–70.

Grimke, Francis J. "Second Marriage of Frederick Douglass." *Journal of Negro History* 19 (July 1934): 324–29

Higginbotham, A. L. Jr., and Barbara Kopytoff. "Racial Purity and Interracial Sex in the Law of Colonial and Antebellum Virginia." In *Interracialism in Black-White Intermarriage in American History, Literature and Law,* edited by Werner Sollors, 81–139. New York: Oxford University Press, 2000.

Landfair, Tillar Hutchens. "Life and Times of Sheriff Bill Preston." *Programs of the Desha County Historical Society* 1 (1974): 37–42.

Lanier, Robert A. The History of the Memphis and Shelby County Bar. [Memphis?]: n.p., 1981.

Lovett, Laura L. "'Africans and Cherokee by Choice': Race and Resistance under Legalized Segregation." In *Confounding the Color Line: The Indian-Black Experience in North America,* edited by James F. Brooks, 192–222. Lincoln: University of Nebraska Press.

Martin, Joel W. "'My Grandmother Was a Cherokee Princess': Representations of Indians in Southern History." In *Dressing in Feathers: The Construction of the Indian in American Popular Culture,* edited by Elizabeth S. Bird, 129–48. Boulder, CO: Westview Press, 1996.

Merritt, James. "Arkansas City, A Natural Steamboat Landing." *Desha County Historical Society Quarterly* 16 (1991): 13–16.

Metheny, Kelley. "Interracial Marriage and Cohabitation in Pulaski County, Arkansas, 1870–1900." *Pulaski County Historical Review,* 44 (Summer 1996): 30–42.

Moneyhon, Carl H. "Black Politics in Arkansas during the Gilded Age, 1876–1900." *Arkansas Historical Quarterly,* 44 (Autumn 1985): 222–45.

Moore, Grover, "Separation from the Union." In *A History of Mississippi,* volume 1, edited by Richard McLemore,

420–46. Jackson: University & College Press of Mississippi, 1973.

Murrell, Amy E. "Of Necessity and Public Benefit." In *Southern Families at War: Loyalty and Conflict in the Civil War South,* edited by Catherine Clinton, 77–99. New York: Oxford University Press, 2000.

Palmer, Paul C. "Miscegenation as an Issue in the Arkansas Constitutional Convention of 1868." *Arkansas Historical Quarterly* 24 (Spring–Winter 1965): 99–119.

Porter, Carolyn, K. "Henry Thane." *Programs of the Desha County Historical Society* 19 (1995): 16–27.

Robinson, Armstead L. "'Plans Dat Comed from God': Institution Building and the Emergence of Black Leadership in Reconstruction Memphis." In *Toward A New South? Studies in Post–Civil War Southern Communities,* edited by Orville V. Burton and Robert C. McMath Jr., 71–102. Westport: Greenwood Press, 1982.

Robinson, Charles F. "'Most Shamefully Common': Arkansas and Miscegenation." *Arkansas Historical Quarterly* 55 (Fall 2001): 265–83.

Rousey, Dennis C. "Yellow Fever and Black Policemen in Memphis: A Post-Reconstruction Anomaly: *Journal of Southern History* 51 (August 1985): 357–74.

Schwartz, Marie J. "'At Noon, Oh How I Ran': Breastfeeding and Weaning on Plantation and Farm in Antebellum Virginia and Alabama. In *Discovering the Women in Slavery,* edited by Patricia Morton, 241–59. Athens: University of Georgia Press, 1996.

St. Hilaire, Joseph M. "The Negro Delegates in the Constitutional Convention of 1868: A Group Profile." *Arkansas Historical Quarterly* 33 (Spring 1974): 43–64.

Books

Baggett, James A. *The Scalawags: Southern Dissenters in the Civil War and Reconstruction.* Baton Rouge: Louisiana State University Press, 2003.

Bardaglio, Peter W. *Reconstructing the Household: Families, Sex, and Law in the Nineteenth Century South.* Chapel Hill: University of North Carolina Press, 1995.

Bercaw, Nancy. *Gendered Freedoms: Race, Rights and the Politics of Household in the Delta, 1861–1875.* Gainsville: University of Florida Press, 2003.

Blassingame, John. *The Slave Community: Plantation Life in the Antebellum South.* New York: Oxford University Press, 1979.

Bontemps, Arna. *Free At Last: The Life of Frederick Douglass.* New York: Dodd, Mead & Co., 1971.

Brown, Kathleen M. *Good Wives, Nasty Wenches and Anxious Patriarchs: Gender, Race and Power in Colonial Virginia.* Chapel Hill: University of North Carolina Press, 1985.

Bruce, Jr. Dickson D. *Violence and Culture in the Antebellum South.* Austin: University of Texas, 1979.

Camp, Stephanie. *Closer to Freedom: Enslaved Women and Everyday Resistance in the Plantation South.* Chapel Hill: University of North Carolina press, 2004.

Cartwright, Joseph H. *The Triumph of Jim Crow: Tennessee Race Relations in the 1880s.* Knoxville: University of Tennessee Press, 1981.

Cash, W. J. *The Mind of the South.* New York: Alfred A. Knopf, 1941.

Chambers, William Pitt. *Blood and Sacrifice: The Civil War Journal of a Confederate Soldier.* Edited by Richard A. Baumgartner. Huntington, WV: Blue Acorn Press, 1994.

Cobb, James C. *The Most Southern Place on Earth: The Mississippi Delta and the Roots of Regional Identity.* New York: Oxford University Press, 1992.

Davis, William C. *Look Away! A History of the Confederate States of America.* New York: Free Press, 2002.

DeBlack, Thomas A. *With Fire and Sword: Arkansas, 1861–1874.* Fayetteville: University of Arkansas Press, 2003.

D'Emilio, John, and Estelle B. Freedman. *Intimate Matters: A History of Sexuality on America.* 2nd ed. Chicago: University of Chicago Press, 1997.

Diedrich, Maria. *Love across Color Lines: Ottilie Assing and Frederick Douglass.* New York: Hill and Wang, 1999.

Dobson, James, C. *Marriage under Fire: Why We Must Win This War.* Sisters, OR: Multnomah, 2004.

Dubay, Robert W. John. *Jones Pettus, Mississippi Fire-Eater: His Life and Times, 1813–1867.* Jackson: University Press of Mississippi, 1975.

DuBois, Ellen C., and Lynn Dumenil. *Through Women's Eyes: An American History.* Boston: Bedford/St. Martin's, 2005.

Dunaway, Wilma A. *The African-American Family in Slavery and Emancipation.* New York: Cambridge University Press, 2003.

Duster, Alfreda M., ed. *Crusade for Justice: The Autobiography of Ida B. Wells.* Chicago: University of Chicago Press, 1970.

Edwards, Laura F. *Gendered Strife and Confusion: The Political Culture of Reconstruction.* Urbana: University of Illinois Press, 1997.

Ely, James W. Jr., ed. *A History of the Tennessee Supreme Court.* Knoxville: University of Tennessee Press, 2002.

Foner, Eric. *A Short History of Reconstruction.* New York: Harper & Row, 1990.

Fowler, David H. *Northern Attitudes towards Interracial Marriage: Legislation and Public Opinion in Middle Atlantic States of the Old Northwest, 1780–1930.* New York: Garland Publishing, 1987.

Frankel, Noralee. *Freedom's Women: Black Women and Families in Civil War Era Mississippi.* Bloomington: Indiana University Press, 1999.

Franklin, John Hope. *The Militant South.* New York: Alfred A. Knopf, 1941.

Gatewood, Willard B. *Aristocrats of Color: The Black Elite, 1880–1920.* Fayetteville: University of Arkansas Press, 2000.

Genovese, Eugene D. *Roll, Jordan, Roll: The World the Slaves Made.* New York: Vintage Books, 1974.

Gilmore, Elizabeth. *Gender and Jim Crow: Women and the Politics of White Supremacy in North Carolina,*

1896–1920. Chapel Hill: University of North
Carolina Press, 1996.

Graves, John William. *Town and Country: Race Relations
in an Urban-Rural Context, Arkansas, 1865–1905.*
Fayetteville: University of Arkansas Press, 1990.

Gray, Deborah W. *"'Ar'nt I a Woman?' Female Slaves in the
Plantation South."* Rev. ed. New York: W. W. Norton
and Co., 1999.

Greene, Lorenzo J. *The Negro in Colonial New England.* New
York: Antheneum, 1969.

Gutman, Herbert G. *The Black Family in Slavery and Freedom, 1750–1925.* New York: Vintage Books, 1976.

Hewitt, Janet B., ed. *Supplement to the Official Records of the
Union and Confederate Armies.* Vol. 33. Wilmington,
NC: Broadfoot Publishing Co., 1996.

Horn, Stanley F. *Invisible Empire: The Story of the Ku Klux
Klan, 1866–1871.* 2nd ed. Montclair, NJ: Patterson
Smith, 1969.

Hunter, Tera. *To 'Joy My Freedom: Southern Black Women's
Lives and Labors after the Civil War.* Cambridge:
Harvard University Press, 1997.

Johnston, James H. *Race Relations in Virginia and Miscegenation in the South, 1776–1860.* Amherst: University
of Massachusetts Press, 1970.

Jones, Jaqueline. *Labor of Love, Labor of Sorrow: Black Women,
Work, and the Family from Slavery to the Present.*
New York: Basic Books. 1985.

Jordan, Winthrop D. *White over Black: American Attitudes
toward the Negro, 1550–1812.* New York: W. W.
Norton, 1968.

Kolchin, Peter. *American Slavery, 1619–1877.* New York: Hill and Wang, 1993.

Martin, Waldo E., Jr., *The Mind of Frederick Douglass.* Chapel Hill: University of North Carolina Press, 1970.

McCurry, Stephanie. *Masters of Small Worlds: Yeoman, Households, Gender Relations, and the Political Culture of the Antebellum South Carolina Low Country.* New York: Oxford University Press, 1995.

McLaurin, Melton A. *Celia, a Slave.* Athens: University of Georgia Press, 1991.

McMillen, Sally G. *Southern Women: Black and White in the Old South.* Arlington: Harlan Davidson, 1992.

McNeilly, Donald P. *The Old South Frontier: Cotton Plantations and the Formation of Arkansas, 1819–1861.* Fayetteville: University of Arkansas Press, 2000.

Mitchell, Reid. *Civil War Soldiers: Their Expectations and their Experiences.* New York: Simon & Schuster, 1988.

Moneyhon, Carl H. *The Impact of the Civil War and Reconstruction on Arkansas: Persistence in the Midst of Ruin.* Fayetteville: University of Arkansas Press, 2002.

Ornelas-Struve, Carole M., comp., and Joan Hassell, ed. *Memphis, 1800–1900.* Vol. 3, *Years of Courage, 1870–1900.* New York: Nancy Powers & Co., 1982.

Ownby, Ted. *Subduing Satan: Religion, Recreation, and Manhood in the Rural South, 1865–1920.* Chapel Hill: University of North Carolina Press, 1990.

Pessen, Edward. *Jacksonian America: Society, Personality, and Politics.* Homewood, IL: Dorsey Press, 1969.

Quinn, David B. *The Elizabethans and the Irish.* Ithaca, NY: Cornell University Press, 1966.

Rabinowitz, Howard. *Race Relations in the Urban South, 1865–1890.* New York: Oxford University Press, 1978.

Rainwater, Percy L. *Mississippi: A Storm Center of Secession, 1856–1861.* Baton Rouge, LA: J. E. Ortlieb Printing Co., 1938.

Rawick, George, ed. *The American Slave: A Composite Autobiography.* Supplement, series 1. Westport, CT: Greenwood Publications, 1977.

Restad, Penne L. *Christmas in America: A History.* New York: Oxford University Press, 1995.

Roberts, Bobby, and Carl Moneyhon. *Portraits of Conflict: A Photographic History of Mississippi in the Civil War.* Fayetteville: University of Arkansas Press, 1993.

Robinson, Charles F. *Dangerous Liaisons: Sex and Love in the Segregated South.* Fayetteville: University of Arkansas Press, 2003.

Rothman, Joshua. *Notorious in the Neighborhood: Sex and Families across the Color Line in Virginia, 1787–1861.* Chapel Hill: University of North Carolina Press, 2003.

Rowland, Dunbar. *Military History of Mississippi, 1803–1898.* Madison, MS: Chickasaw Bayou Press, 2003.

Schwartz, Marie J. *Born in Bondage: Growing Up Enslaved in the Antebellum South.* Cambridge, MA: Harvard University Press, 2000.

Sewell, Richard H. *A House Divided: Sectionalism and Civil War, 1848–1865.* Baltimore: Johns Hopkins University Press, 1988.

Sillers, Florence W. *History of Bolivar County.* Jackson, MS: Hederman Brothers, 1948.

Speer, Lonnie R. *Portals to Hell: Military Prisons of the Civil War.* Mechanicsburg, PA: Stackpole Books, 1997.

Tannahill, Reay. *Sex in History.* Rev. ed. Chelsea, MI: Scarborough House, 1992.

Taylor, Alrutheus, A. *The Negro in Tennessee, 1865–1880.* Washington, D.C.: Association for Study of Negro Life and History, 1941.

Wharton, Vernon L. *The Negro in Mississippi, 1865–1890.* New York: Harper & Row, 1965.

White, Richard. *The Middle Ground: Indian, Empires, and Republics in the Great Lake Region, 1650–1815.* New York: Cambridge University Press, 1996.

Williams, Jack. *Dueling in the Old South.* College Station: Texas A&M University Press, 1980.

Wyatt-Brown, Bertram. *Honor and Violence in the Old South.* New York: Oxford University Press, 1986.

———. *The Shaping of Southern Culture: Honor, Grace, and War, 1760s–1880s.* Chapel Hill: University of North Carolina Press, 2001.

Dissertations

Caplinger, Christopher. "Conflict and Community: Racial Segregation in a New South City, 1860–1914." PhD diss., Dept. of History, Vanderbilt University, 2003.

Berkeley, Kathleen C. "'Like a Plague of Locusts': Immigration and Social Change in Memphis Tennessee, 1850–1880." PhD diss., Dept. of History, University of California, 1980.

Davis, Denoral. "Against the Odds: Postbellum Growth and Development in a Southern Black Urban Community, 1865–1900." PhD diss., Dept. of History, State University of New York at Binghamton, 1987.

INDEX

FORSAKING ALL OTHERS
was designed and typeset on a Macintosh computer system using InDesign
software. The body text is set in 10/13 Kepler and display type is set in
Engravers MT. This book was designed and typeset by Chad Pelton,
and manufactured by Thomson-Shore, Inc.